THE ENTRAPMENT OF THE POOR INTO INVOLUNTARY LABOR

Understanding the Worldwide Practice of Modern-Day Slavery

THE ENTRAPMENT OF THE POOR INTO INVOLUNTARY LABOR
Understanding the Worldwide Practice of Modern-Day Slavery

Adel S. Abadeer

With a Foreword by
Karl W. Schweizer

The Edwin Mellen Press
Lewiston•Queenston•Lampeter

Library of Congress Cataloging-in-Publication Data

Abadeer, Adel S.
The entrapment of the poor into involuntary labor : understanding the worldwide
practice of modern-day slavery / Adel S. Abadeer ; with a foreword by Karl Schweizer.
  p. cm.
  [Includes bibliographical references and index.]
  ISBN-13: 978-0-7734-5046-2
  ISBN-10: 0-7734-5046-7
  1. Peonage--India. 2. Human trafficking--India. 3. Poor--India. 4. Slavery--India. 5.
Social justice--Religious aspects--Christianity. I. Title.
  HD4875.I5A48 2008
  331.11'734--dc22
                                                                2008028674

hors série.

A CIP catalog record for this book is available from the British Library.

The Edwin Mellen Press   The Edwin Mellen Press
        Box 450   Box 67
   Lewiston, New York   Queenston, Ontario
   USA 14092-0450   CANADA L0S 1L0

The Edwin Mellen Press, Ltd.
Lampeter, Ceredigion, Wales
UNITED KINGDOM SA48 8LT

Printed in the United States of America

To my mother

Contents

Foreword by Dr. Karl W. Schweizer

Sadly, "human trafficking" or modern day slavery (MDS)—a deplorable remnant of humanity's past—is alive and well; indeed, it has become an alarming scourge, impacting more than 130 nations worldwide. The International Labor Organization has estimated that more than 12 million individuals around the world are victims of bondage; drug related forced labor, sexual exploitation, or other atrocities.[1] According to the American Bar Association, human trafficking generates billions in profits yearly and is "the fastest growing and third largest criminal industry in the world (after the arms and drug trades).[2] Eighty percent of those trafficked across borders are helpless females or children—a global calamity all too often ignored, repressed, or under publicized.

In this stimulating, well written and conceptually innovative—not to mention timely—work, Dr. Abadeer provides, for the first time, researched-based criteria for an effective intervention strategy which counters MDS practices realistically at the local, national, and international levels.

Sensitive to the inherently complex components and deep historic/cultural roots of MDS phenomena, Dr. Abadeer formulates his remedial strategy accordingly, drawing for insights on political science, sociology, psychology, economics, anthropology, as well as Christian teaching. The latter, especially, given the book's academic genre, is an unusual perspective but one very much needed in this post-modernist age; one that provides us with a vision of history and life infinite in hope and redemptive possibilities. With passion and perception, Dr. Abadeer reminds us that Christians are not mere spectators in the

---

[1] Trafficking in Persons Report (US State Department, 2007).

[2] ABA Journal, March 2006, pp. 34-36, In Touch Magazine, (July 2008), pp. 13-14.

drama of world calamities but must use their spiritual energy to combat the true source of these problems, the crisis of mankind's separation from fellow man and, above all, God—the failure of love. By reinserting the notion of Divine love as the ultimate measure of our conduct, the book, using the MDS paradigm, shows how to overcome spiritual muteness and moral paralysis. As such, from the author's viewpoint, "the immediacy of pain and sorrow, the primacy of tragedy and suffering in human life, may be transmuted into a spiritual and moral triumph."[3]

On the more practical, applied side, Dr. Abadeer employs international economical analysis to confront the textured nuances of MDS's manifestations around the world; third world countries in particular. Recognizing that formal institutions play a critical role in creating the culturally sanctioned conditions conducive to MDS practices, Dr. Abadeer advocates intervention efforts that recognize indigenous cultural norms, address the institutions—the governance structure—responsive to MDS precepts, cover immediate and long-term targets and objectives, and consider the strength and limitations of each level, form and scope of intervention. Only intervention on such levels, the book demonstrates convincingly can ultimately negate the power structure, inherited beliefs and traditions in those societies and communities (i.e. India) where the unempowered and marginalized are condemned to victim status. Applied rigorously this approach represents a unique example of how scholarly research, enriched by wider spiritual awareness, can be transmuted to impact the actual course of events. Here the author has moved "from a stance towards the world that emphasizes detached observation and analysis to a stance in which observation is increasingly mixed with participation, analysis with judgment and advice."[4]

---

[3] H. Butterfield, International Conflict in the 20th Century, (London, 1960), p. 9.

[4] N. Glazer, "Theory and Practice in the Social Sciences," Chronicle of Higher Education, July 31, 1978, p. 28.

While further research still needs to be done on MDS in its full complexity, Dr. Abadeer in toto has provided valuable pointers for the direction of such work, has expanded our knowledge of the myriad factors facilitating MDS practices, and has shown how the proper application of this knowledge builds foundations for effective intervention and remedies. We can hope for no more than that statesmen and policymakers, not just academic specialists, will obtain this book, read it and, ideally, learn from it.

Karl W. Schweizer, Ph.D. (Cambridge)
F.R.HIST.S.
Professor of History,l Rutgers/NJIT

Preface

Modern-day slavery (MDS) is one of many manifestations and outcomes resulting from the so-called "Fall" of humanity. It is one of the most alarming practices of human rights violations that still exist in the twenty-first century, especially in some less developed countries (LDCs), where significant numbers of poor and vulnerable people are being transformed into victims, and coerced into different forms of enslavement. Modern-day slavery is gaining greater national and international interest and attention, due to the increasing trend toward globalization and the dissemination of information regarding the occurrence of this appalling and widespread phenomenon in certain LDCs.

The new institutional economics analysis considers institutions to be humanly devised constraints that structure human interactions. The three major categories of institutions are the informal institutions (e.g., culture[5], norms[6], beliefs, traditions, myths, expectations), the formal rules (e.g., polity, judiciary, laws, and regulations), and the governance structure of transactions (or the costs of making transactions). This approach opens up a genuinely interdisciplinary analysis, involving political science, religion, sociology, and psychology, as well

---

[5] Culture, throughout this book, loosely consists of "regularities in the behavior, internal and external, of the members of society, excluding those regularities which are purely hereditary" (Akerlof, 1976, p. 600). According to UNESCO, culture is a "set of distinctive spiritual, material, intellectual and emotional features of society or a social group, and that it encompasses, in addition to art and literature, lifestyles, ways of living together, value systems, traditions and beliefs" (UNESCO, 2002, paragraph 5). It involves very low levels of intentions, applies to very large groups, sometimes the entire society, and it serves as a check on opportunism (Williamson, 1993, pp. 476-477)

[6] Norms generally refer to socially-enforced rules regarding how people should behave in different situations. According to J. S. Coleman, "Norms are expectation about one's own actions and/or that of others which express what action is right or what action is wrong" (Coleman, 1987, pp. 142-42).

as economics. In addition, it ascribes an important role to ideology and history, where the present and future are connected to the past through the continuity of society's institutions.

Institutions play crucial roles in spreading (or eradicating) practices such as modern-day slavery, based on the societal reward and penalty systems that accompany such institutions. As the analysis in this book shows, MDS practices tend to spread in societies and communities where inherited beliefs and traditions sanction certain social behaviors and structures, and separate and/or marginalize certain groups such as India's Scheduled Castes and Scheduled Tribes (SC/ST), and women. Existing polity, judiciary, laws, and regulations usually reflect the power structure and the dominance of the beneficiaries of inherited beliefs and traditions (e.g., the upper Hindu castes), at the expense of the vulnerable and marginalized SC/ST and women. Additionally, the governance structure of transactions usually works against the enslaveables (the vulnerable and marginalized population groups), since they are less informed, more desperate, entrapped, coerced, and lack viable support systems (government or private), and are intentionally marginalized in order to accept their fate as MDS victims. MDS perpetrators utilize the above factors to sustain their practices, avoid and outlast intervention attempts, and exploit the influence of interest groups and corrupt government officials.

Institutional economic analysis outlines the criteria for effective interventions against modern-day slavery. Effective interventions should address the causes, processes, and symptoms of modern-day slavery, and must respond to the perpetrators' complex schemes and tactics, used in entrapping the victims and perpetuating MDS practices. Consequently, effective interventions should take place at the local, national, and international levels, and should cover immediate/short-term to long-term targets and objectives, taking into consideration the strengths and limitations of each level, form, and scope of intervention.

This book is an attempt to shed light on the complex MDS phenomena in LDCs, utilizing the new institutional economic analysis, with India as a case study. It underscores the crucial role of the surrounding institutional environment (the informal and formal institutions and their governance), and shows how our understanding of a complex phenomenon such as modern-day slavery can be improved through the application of the appropriate new institutional economic analysis. The new institutional economic approach utilizes the relationships and linkages to other disciplines such as history, sociology, psychology, anthropology, and political science. However, the book does not (and cannot) cover all issues associated with a full understanding of modern-day slavery; it serves as an invitation, however, to other scholars for further intellectual exchanges.

Due to increasing foreign/international attention and interventions against modern-day slavery in LDCs, the book proposes a set of special considerations to accompany foreign and international interventions and enhance their effectiveness. The book begins and concludes with a Biblical perspective on modern-day slavery and highlights foundations for effective Christian interventions and remedies.

The book also explains the continuation of traditional slavery, yet in a different format and in accordance with the modernization of societies, showing that modern-day slavery is an industry that adapts easily to changes in the cultural, legal, social, political and economic structures and environments in different societies and globally. It also sheds some light on factors that lead to the spreading of MDS practices and proposes interventions that consider these factors. Further, this book serves as an invitation for continued studies and research in topics that seem overlooked, primarily due to the distressing nature of modern-day slavery and its voiceless and defenseless victims.

The interdisciplinary institutional economics approach sheds light on crucial factors and processes that have been ignored in other studies of modern-day slavery. Understanding the process of making a slave is vital for designing and proposing effective interventions against MDS practices, both to prevent those practices from taking place and to pre-empt every stage of that process. This interdisciplinary approach should appeal to a larger audience such as those involved with human rights organizations, relief programs, community development programs in LDCs, and so forth. The book considers MDS from a Christian perspective that sees it as a consequence of the Fall, which is in need of redemption. The characters and means for such redemption are explored and analyzed.

The analysis in the book is also applicable (with needed specific modifications) to the state of minority and marginalized groups in LDCs, who suffer because of their affiliation with vulnerable population groups. These groups are identified through inherited/existing physical or social markers, such as ethnicity, religion, gender, and caste.

Modern-Day Slavery and Child Labor

This book is not meant to cover child labor per se. MDS practices differ from normal child labor since the common thread here is the forced participation of MDS victims through, for example, bonded labor and forced prostitution. This difference is vital to the understanding of modern-day slavery in LDCs, and separates it from the child labor problem in LDCs. The topic of child labor has already gained national and international academic interest and coverage (and still needs more analysis and coverage). However, this book highlights the fact that MDS victims include adults (especially women) in addition to children, and that women have a significant share and burden as MDS victims, especially in the sex sector, including the ongoing phenomena of human trafficking.

Structure of the Book

The book consists of six chapters: Chapter 1 serves as an introduction to the MDS phenomenon in LDCs. It covers the importance of new institutional economics analysis of modern-day slavery, the widespread practices of modern-day slavery in LDCs, the use of modern-day slavery in India as the case study of the book, and MDS statistics. Chapter 2 outlines and analyzes the enslavement process: the process of transforming the most vulnerable amongst the enslaveables into actual MDS victims, and the perpetrators' schemes to perpetuate MDS practices for the purpose of maximizing their gain from enslaving the victims, typically referred to as the "enslavement rent." Chapter 3 surveys the institutional environment with regard to the classification of institutions, their major attributes, interdependence, their relevance and significance to modern-day slavery in LDCs, and a new institutional economic analysis of modern-day slavery that helps to analyze the critical variables and dynamics that support MDS practices. Chapter 4 utilizes the analysis in Chapter 3 to identify and recommend proper anti-MDS interventions and remedies, in addition to providing special considerations for effective interventions and remedies. Chapter 5 develops a Biblical perspective on effective Christian intervention and remedies against modern-day slavery. The book concludes with a summary and conclusion in Chapter 6.

Recommended Audiences

This book provides a new approach and insights toward a better understanding of modern-day slavery and proposes more effective policies and interventions by international human rights organizations and national policy makers, directors, and public servants in governmental human rights agencies.

International and national civil society organizations (CSOs) and non-government organizations (NGOs) that are interested in eradicating modern-day slavery and other forms of human rights' violations in LDCs, especially in the poor and marginalized communities, should have great interest in the analysis and recommendations in this book.

This book should be useful to Christian institutions, especially those involved with training and orientation programs for missionaries and relief agents. It provides a better understanding of the key institutional factors that are usually ignored or overlooked in addressing modern-day slavery (and other related practices, such as the marginalization and prejudice towards indigenous people, women, and rural residents), in LDCs. The book also provides Christian foundations and criteria for effective and redemptive interventions that serve the interests of these marginalized communities, and may serve to eradicate MDS practices in the process.

The book should also be useful as supplemental reading in higher academic institutions for economics majors (economic development, poverty, institutional economics, and economics of LDCs); international relations majors, international development majors; and, as required or strongly recommended reading in courses on human rights.

Finally, the interdisciplinary approach of new institutional economics regarding modern-day slavery should attract larger audiences to the book (e.g., economics, political science, international relations, third world studies), in addition to institutions that are involved or interested in human rights and human rights violations.

Acknowledgments

I would like to express my special appreciation to my colleagues at Calvin College for their input and help, especially Professors Roland Hoksbergen and John Tiemstra for their insightful comments and suggestions on an earlier version of this book, and Professors Shirley Roels, Kurt Schaefer, and Andrew Samuel for their support and valued comments. I am also grateful for valuable comments I received on parts of this book presented as papers at various conferences.

I would like to thank Ms. Susan Camp of the Economics Department and the Calvin College Rhetoric Center for their help with proofreading parts of the manuscript. I also thank Ms. Judith Pereira for copy editing and proofreading the final version of this book and Ms. Susan Lohmeyer for indexing it.

Finally, special thanks to students in my course Human Rights and Modern-Day Slavery in the Twenty-First Century, January 2003 at Calvin College, for their comments and contributions.

Chapter 1

Introduction

Woe to those who make unjust laws, to those who issue oppressive decrees, to deprive the poor of their rights and withhold justice from the oppressed of my people, making widows their prey and robbing the fatherless. (Isaiah 10:1-2)

Do not mistreat an alien or oppress him, for you were aliens in Egypt. Do not take advantage of a widow or an orphan… If you lend money to one of my people among you who is needy, do not be like a moneylender; charge him no interest. If you take your neighbor's cloak as a pledge, return it to him by sunset, because his cloak is the only covering he has for his body. What else will he sleep in? When he cries out to me, I will hear, for I am compassionate. (Exodus 22:21-22, 25-27)

Speak up for those who cannot speak for themselves, for the rights of all who are destitute. Speak up and judge fairly; defend the rights of the poor and needy. (Proverbs 31:8-9)

On the threshold of this twenty-first century, certain human rights violations, such as slavery, are thought to be matters of the past. Yet, significant numbers of the vulnerable and marginalized population groups in less developed countries (LDCs) – especially young children and women – are being transformed, and forced into different forms of enslavement. This phenomenon, which is known as modern-day slavery (MDS), is occurring nowadays despite international and national declarations, treaties, and interventions against modern-day slavery. It is a violation of human rights that represents one of the most alarming and unjust practices of our modern world – a practice still alive and widespread today.

Some may wonder, "Why modern-day slavery?" In a fallen world (i.e., in Biblical terms, the world occurring after Adam and Eve's fall from grace), a more proper question should be "Why not?" Modern-day slavery is one of many manifestations and outcomes resulting from this so-called Fall of humanity. Dire poverty, marginalization of, and discrimination against certain population groups, limitless greed, and lack of concern for others' well-being, all feed the depredation of MDS perpetrators and their collaborators at the expense of the vulnerable and marginalized population groups, the enslaveables.

MDS victims are typically very poor (or ultra poor[7]), illiterate, vulnerable, and marginalized, and are more likely to stay poor for extended periods. Most of these victims are women and children from marginalized and disconnected communities, who are victims of institutional discrimination – discrimination enforced and embedded through informal social constraints such as myths, dogmas, ideologies, traditions, and self-imposed codes of conduct. These informal institutions provide the informal bases for MDS practices, in terms of segregating and marginalizing certain population group(s) according to their beliefs, religion, race, ethnic backgrounds, and so forth. In addition, they are also the victims of corrupt or ineffective formal rules (or formal institutions) such as polity, judiciary, laws, regulations, and complex/imperfect governance structure of transactions (explained in detail in Chapter 3). The enslaveables are typically unaware of the imperfect nature of transactions, the terms of such transactions, and of the perpetrators' schemes and processes of enslavement. Moreover, they lack access to viable alternative sources such as free schooling, employment, credit facilities, legal services, and welfare programs. The perpetrators, in contrast, exploit the incompleteness of contracts or transactions, in terms of the significant information gap between them and their potential victims (the enslaveables), and the desperate state of the enslaveables that results from their ignorance, vulnerability, and the absence of viable alternatives.

---

[7] The ultra poor refer to the poor who live with few, if any, assets and have very limited chances to earn income. They typically survive below the basic human needs (e.g., food, water, clothing, shelter, and sanitation) and earn their income as subsistence laborers, beggars, or through participation in scavenging activities. For more definitions and measurement of the ultra poor, see UNDP (undated and 2004b).

Modern-day slavery is a relatively complex topic to research and analyze for many reasons. The intricate institutional structure in each society and the interdependencies of informal institutions (e.g., norms, traditions, religions), formal institutions (e.g., laws, regulations, and their enforcement), and the governance structure of the transactions (e.g., the cost of governing transactions and contracts) play crucial roles in MDS practices. The large number of participants in MDS practices and the "forced" participation of MDS victims also contribute to the complexity of the analysis. Then, there are the dual roles of some participants, such as public servants, police officers, and judges, who are supposed to intervene on behalf of MDS victims and prosecute MDS perpetrators, yet, who may also intervene on behalf of MDS perpetrators and collaborate with them, as well. The rise of national and international interests to eradicate modern-day slavery – or to participate and benefit from it – must also be taken into consideration. Lastly, modern-day slavery manifests itself in many forms, such as chattel slavery, debt bondage, forced labor, human trafficking, and sex-sector slavery (e.g., forced prostitution, pornography, and pedophile slavery).

1. Why a New Institutional Economic Analysis of Modern-Day Slavery?

> Traditional economics that is preoccupied with formal modeling and abstract has failed to come to grips with the daily reality of poor people's lives. Martha Nussbaum (2000, p. xv)

> [T]he role that political, legal and social institutions play in framing this process of learning and adjustment takes on a necessary urgency that is absent in the institutionally antiseptic neoclassical theory of rational agency where the behavioral postulates in the intellectual framework do all the heavy intellectual lifting. Scott Beaulier, et al. (2005, p. 222)

This book utilizes the new institutional economic analysis that encompasses the appropriate analytical tools to research complex phenomena such as modern-day slavery. New institutional economics builds on, modifies, and extends the neoclassical economic framework. It retains and builds on the neoclassical fundamental assumptions of scarcity and competition, but rejects the assumptions of complete and symmetric information, no transaction costs,[8] and the unimportance (or neutrality) of institutions (North, 1998). New institutional economics takes into consideration that information is incomplete and asymmetric, the presence of positive transaction costs, and the prevalence of continuing relationships between parties to transactions (Akerlof, 1976, p. 599; Hirschman, 1982, pp. 1474-74; Sykuta and Cook, 2001, p. 1274). It also opens the terrain of interdisciplinary inquiry such as history, religion, politics, sociology, anthropology, as well as economics. Therefore, it provides multidisciplinary insight into social problems. It also ascribes an important role to ideas and ideologies that explain the perpetuation of what seem to be irrational phenomena or social dilemmas, such as modern-day slavery in some LDCs.

In addition, new institutional economic analysis encompasses the panoply of cultural characteristics used by anthropologists and sociologists to describe a society, where individual identities and social backgrounds do matter, reconciling the *homo-economicous* and the *homo-sociologicus* behaviors (Akerlof, 1976, p. 600; Platteau, 1994a, p. 538). *Homo-economicous* behavior is guided by instrumental rationality, pulled by the prospect of future rewards, adaptive to changing circumstances – almost on the lookout for improvement – and easily caricatured as a self-contained and asocial atom. In contrast, *homo-sociologicus* behavior is dictated by social norms, pushed from behind by quasi-inertial forces, is insensitive to circumstances – sticking to prescribed behavior even if new and apparently better options become available – and easily caricatured as the mindless plaything of social forces (Elster, 1989, p. 99).

---

[8] Transaction cost refers to "the value of real resources used to effectuate a transfer of ownership rights. It differs from production cost, which refers to "the values of real resources used up in the production of a good or service once ownership rights to inputs have been obtained." (Kaufman, 2007, p. 26).

Social dilemmas such as modern-day slavery occur when choices made by 'rational' individuals (the enslaveables, MDS victims, and MDS perpetrators) yield outcomes that are socially irrational, where the perpetrators can force their victims to participate in MDS practices (Harris, Hunter, and Lewis, 1998), under certain institutional environments that include discriminating informal norms and traditions (developed over an evolutionary process of gradual feedback and adjustments), as well as distorted formal rules, such as legislation, regulations, and law enforcement. All serve the interest of those with bargaining power to perpetuate certain rules and create new ones at the expense of the victims of such norms and rules (Kasper and Streit, 1998; North, 1998), and explain the presence and perpetuation of social dilemma such as modern-day slavery in some LDCs.

Furthermore, new institutional economic analysis takes into account the incomplete nature of contracts and transactions due to incomplete and asymmetrical information, which in turn results in the participants' bounded rationality,[9] and the cost of governing transactions and contracts becomes the rule rather than the exception (contrary to neoclassical economics). New institutional economics becomes pertinent as soon as we take into consideration the use of fraud and deceit by individuals (such as MDS perpetrators and their collaborators) to achieve their self-interest ends (Platteau, 1994a, p. 540). Under these circumstances, MDS perpetrators can entrap the enslaveables, who are typically very poor, weary, and uninformed, in MDS schemes and transform them into MDS victims. Douglass North (1990) describes such institutional frameworks – not as inefficient – but, as efficient in making a society more unproductive and in serving the interest of certain groups (e.g., upper castes and MDS perpetrators) at the expense of others (e.g., SC/ST, the enslaveables, and MDS victims). Akerlof

---

[9] Bounded rationality refers to individuals who make use of a subset of the decision's attributes in their decisions, rather than taking all attributes of the decision into consideration, due to their limited/imperfect information and cognitive capacity. For further analysis, see Korobkin (2003), and Williamson (1981, 2000).

(1976, p. 600) highlighted the role of indicators in making exchanges. Some indicators owe their existence purely to social conventions rather than to economic information, in, almost all, conventional economic models. In the case of the caste system in India, individuals' behavior toward others is predicted by their respective caste status.

Platteau (1994a) highlights the importance of both social and traditional norms, especially in LDCs, "In traditional or preindustrial societies individuals occupy definite positions in the social matrix and the functions which they fulfill are thus determined by a priori definition of what they socially are (most commonly, from as early as their birth)" (p. 538). He also compares the appeal of market transactions and actions that are implied by interest-guided behavior to those triggered by violent, wild, and destructive passions, such as those ensuing from the quest for social leverage and political clout, or by religious, ethnic, and other kinds of deeply-involved feelings. In such environments, minority ethnic groups act in accordance with a priori social norms that define their social identity (p. 538).

Lastly, while the neoclassical economic model defines the rights and duties of abstract agents who are treated as strictly equal, new institutional economics is more relevant in defining the rights and duties of agents based on their personal histories and peculiar circumstances (Platteau 1994a, p. 539). New institutional economics is not confined to the neoclassical models of selfish individuals who are incapable of malevolence and who abstain from any dishonest act (or, even if individuals desire to behave dishonestly, the cost of dishonest behavior is too high, due to perfect information and transparency and the costless enforcement of the law). In such an environment, it is not possible to behave dishonestly, however intense the desire to so act (pp. 540-41). New institutional economics extends the analysis to cover dishonest acts by people who are capable of malevolence in environments associated with imperfect and asymmetric information and corrupt formal rules, such as corrupt governments, absence of law, and or ineffective enforcement of laws, such that dishonest behaviors can be rewarding.

The enslaveables' desperation and lack of viable alternatives (such as educations, loans, employment) versus the MDS perpetrators' strategic behaviors, knowledge, and investment in schemes to exploit the enslaveables' vulnerability and gain at their expense by entrapping them into MDS practices, presents a typical MDS situation in certain LDC communities. Examples of MDS perpetrators' schemes include offering the enslaveables immediate relief (or a promise of immediate relief) such as loans, cash advances, or employment offers, knowing that these desperate enslaveables cannot afford to reject such offers. Platteau (1994a) refers to these schemes: "In virtually all-real world economic exchanges the scope of cheating is present if only because there exists a time-lag, however brief, between each agent performing his side of the exchanges" (p. 541). MDS perpetrators typically offer their help to the enslaveables first, and then trap them into MDS practice schemes afterwards.

2. Modern-Day Slavery and Less Developed Countries (LDCs)

Although some forms of modern-day slavery can exist in certain developed countries, it is more widespread in LDCs for the following reasons:

1. Poverty is widespread in LDCs. Many people, especially in the marginalized communities, still live below or barely at the subsistence levels.

2. Dual societies are prevalent, in terms of the coexistence of mutually exclusive groups (such as majority and ethnic or religious minority groups, the affluent and the extreme poor) and different degrees of superiority and inferiority among various population groups in the same country.[10] Biased government policies against marginalized

---

[10] Todaro and Smith (2006, pp. 117-118).

communities exist (based on their races, ethnic backgrounds, religions, etc.).

3. Embedded informal norms and traditions that permit, or do not effectively reject, the abuse of certain population groups are also prevalent.

4. The absence or ineffective presence of formal rules (e.g., statutory laws, common laws, and regulations, and their enforcements) that protect the enslaveables' human rights, which in turn invites the perpetrators to exploit the enslaveables' vulnerability.

5. Modern-day slavery is a 'convenient' and low-cost means of illegal services, such as forced prostitution (including pedophilia, pornography), or a way of providing workers for hazardous and unhealthy production processes (e.g., brassware, hand-knotted wool carpets, explosive fireworks, hand-blown glass bangles, and hand broken quarried stones).

6. Modern-day slavery is the more preferred, if not the only, way to produce certain goods and services that can only be provided by children. Examples include pedophilia (where pre-pubescent children are coerced to satisfy the adult customers' sexual advances or acts); the production of handmade goods such as hand-spun scarves, carpets, *beedis* (hand-rolled cigarettes), hand-dipped matches (which depend on the soft and tender touch of children's small fingers); and, services by women, such as forced prostitution (U.S. DOS 2003a, Section 6d; UNICEF 2004).

7. MDS practices arise when similar options, such as prostitution and pedophilia, are illegal or otherwise constrained.

8. MDS industries are highly mobile. They operate like hit-and-run firms, without verifiable business addresses, registration, or legal identification, to avoid inspections and subsequent penalties and other

punishments.[11] They typically operate with relatively low overhead costs, primitive tools, and high labor-intensive technologies that require very little, or no, experience.

9. MDS practices, regardless of their gruesome or appalling nature, may be of less importance to LDC governments, given the many problems (e.g., economic, political, and social problems and crises) that LDC governments face, on one hand, and the governments' limited resources and widespread corruption in many LDCs, on the other.

3. India: The Case Study

India is an excellent example for analyzing modern-day slavery in LDCs for many reasons. It is one of the world's oldest civilizations, more than 5000 years old, with rich ethnic, religious, and cultural diversity. Of the 1065 million Indians, 72 percent are of Indo-Aryan ethnicity, 25 percent Dravidian, and three percent Mongoloid and others. There are 17 major languages, including 15 national languages, and 1500 dialects spoken in 28 states, and seven centrally administered Union Territories, where some states' boundaries have been drawn along linguistic lines (Embassy of India). 81.3 percent of Indians are Hindu, followed by 13 percent Muslims, 2.3 percent Christians, 1.9 percent Sikhs, and 2.5 percent other religions, mostly Buddhist, Jain, and Parsi.[12] There is no country with greater diversity and plurality in the world (Nussbaum, 2000, p. 24).

---

[11] A hit-and-run firm typically enters the market fast, when the profit level is unusually high, to take advantage of such high profit, and then exit the market, before the existing firms react to it. A typical MDS firm takes advantage of the lack of effective enforcement of the law, or the usual delay in law enforcement against MDS practices due to the typical time lags associated with government/bureaucracy responses to MDS practices, government corruption, or lack of resources, which are prevalent in LDCs. The MDS firm leaves or relocates when effective government interventions (or credible threats of intervention) against MDS practices takes place.

[12] See CIA (undated) and The World Bank (undated).

India falls into the middle of LDCs in terms of its social and economic performance, according to most international classifications. According to the United Nations (U.N.) 2006 Human Development Report (UNDP), India ranked 114th (out of 177 countries) in gross domestic product (GDP) per capita of purchasing power parity (PPP), US$ 3,139 in 2004.[13] It ranked 121st in life expectancy at birth of 63.8 years; 127th in school enrollment ratio of 62 percent; and, 107th in adult literacy rate of 61%. With a Human Development Index (HDI[14]) of 0.611, India ranked 126th, below LDCs' average HDI of 0.679 and the world average of 0.741. On the other hand, according to the UNDP's Human Poverty Index (HPI-1),[15] which focuses on the most deprived, India ranked 55th out of 102 LDCs, with a score of 31.3 percent. The probability of not surviving to age 40 was 16.6 percent; adult illiteracy was 39 percent; the percentage of the population without sustainable access to an improved water sources was 14 percent; and the percentage of children (under age 5) underweight for their age was 47 percent. Only 79 percent of first grade students in India will reach the fifth grade. That fact, coupled with a 90 percent net primary education enrollment ratio (UNDP, 2006, Table 12), makes millions of India's children (mostly the poor, who live in slums, shantytowns, or marginalized rural areas) more vulnerable, adding them to the enslaveable pool.

---

[13] That is about 66 percent of LDCs average of $4,775, and 36 percent of the world average of $8,833. Purchasing power parity (PPP) accounts for the differences in costs of living across countries. PPP US$1 has the same purchasing power in the domestic economy as $1 in the United States (UNDP, 2006).

[14] HDI is an equally-weighted average of three socioeconomic criteria: longevity (measured by life expectancy at birth), income per capita (adjusted for the PPP to reflect the different cost of living in different countries, and the diminishing benefit from income as income level rises), and knowledge (measured by adult literacy combined with school enrollment) (UNDP, 2006, pp. 394-95).

[15] HPI-1 is the equally weighted index of the following three criteria of socioeconomic deprivation: probability at birth of not surviving to age 40, adult illiteracy rate, and the combined percentage of population without sustainable access to improved water sources and percentage of underweight children. The highest HPI-1 corresponds to the poorest LDCs (UNDP, 2006, p. 395).

According to Platteau (1994b, p. 797), Indian society and other south Asian societies, "remain under the strong influence of traditional patterns of social relations, in particular the principle of the primacy of family and caste relationships. Under these circumstance, it is not surprising that rights and obligations associated with these patterns still tend to predominate over the rules and norms rooted in the abstract individual (as opposed to the concrete person) which are the typical products of western history."

Embedded beliefs and traditions play crucial roles in MDS practices in India due to the relatively rigid and exclusive Hindu caste system (or Hindu social order), with predetermined and inherited social, religious, cultural, and economic rights for each caste. The Hindu caste system places 251 million people (24.4 percent of the Indian population, according to the Census of India, 2001) in Scheduled Castes and Scheduled Tribes (SC/ST), also known as the *Dalits* (which means broken people), out of and far below the Hindu social order. Ostracized, the SC/ST are considered 'unclean', in contrast to the 'clean' upper castes, and are socially boycotted and separated at the bottom of the Hindu social order (Kolenda, 1966; Guru, 2004). The social separation and marginalization of SC/ST heighten their vulnerability and exposure to discrimination and atrocities, including MDS practices, especially among SC/ST women and their dependents. Nearly one-half of SC/ST lives below the poverty line, compared to one third of the rest of the population, based on 1993-94 data (Thorat, 2002). Recent studies indicate that intercaste disparity continues, 50 years after the India's Independence in 1947, underlying the overall disparity between SC/ST compared to the "Other" population in terms of consumption expenditure, asset/land holding, and levels of education (Deshpande, 2000; Unni, 2001). Furthermore, gender discrimination and the subordination of women are still deeply embedded in the Indian/Hindu traditions, and these norms deepen the burden of Dalit women.[16]

Gender discrimination and subordination of women vary according to religions and location, being more prevalent in the Northern states (Das Gupta, et al., 2000). Some rural communities continue to argue against education for girls (beyond the second or third grades), the same way that their grandparents argued earlier on. Girls leave their parents and move to their in-laws to do housework and bear children, soon forgetting what they learn in school because they do not have use for it (Luschinsky, 1966, p. 68). Overall, in 2004, women lag behind in literacy rates (48 percent; 65 percent of male's rate) and school enrollment (female enrollments in primary and tertiary education were about 94 percent, and 66 percent of male's rates, respectively). In addition, female estimated earned income is about 31 percent of male income (PPP US$ 1,471 for a female, and 4,723 for a male) (UNDP, 2006, Table 24). Consequently, there is some disparity in India's Human Development Index (HDI). With an HDI of .611 in 2004, India was ranked 120 out of 177 countries. However, when the Gender-related Development Index (GDI), a modified HDI that takes into consideration the inequalities in achievement between men and women, was included, India was ranked 96th out of 136 countries, with a GDI of .591 in 2004 (UNDP, 2006, Tables 1 and 24). The gender gaps in literacy, school enrollment, access to health services, and earned income draw more women (and their dependents) toward the pool of the most vulnerable (i.e., the enslaveables).[17]

The prevalence of government corruption, especially low-level local corruption in rural areas, provides a safer (or less-risky) environment for illegal practices such as modern-day slavery. According to Transparency International,

---

[16] Dalit women have been specific targets of violence and sexual abuse in many states in India, e.g., Haryana (Chakma, 2007, p. 65).

India's Corruption Perception Index (CPI) of 3.3 in 2006 (ranked 74th out of 163) placed India among the countries with a high level of corruption.[18] Generally, government corruption, at both upper and lower levels, serves the interest of the powerful and influential, at the expense of the poor, especially the marginalized groups, e.g., SC/ST.

In spite of the above, India has experienced continued and significant social and economic advancements, such as the reduction in poverty rate, rising per capita income, remarkable socio-economic development, and an increase in the standard of living.[19] Additionally, governments, especially at the national and state levels, have intervened frequently with subsequent amendments and implementation of more effective methods of intervention to eliminate all forms of discrimination against SC/ST and women and children (Goonesekere, 2001). The National Child Labor Project (NCLP), 2004, is an example of government intervention (in collaboration with the U.S. Department of Labor and the International Labor Organization (ILO)) to combat child labor and to eliminate the worst forms of child labor. This project assisted working children in 3700

---

[17] Examples of singling out Dalit women for harassment are reported by the United States Department of State (U.S. DOS) (2006a, Section 5), and Human Rights Watch (1999, Chapter 9).

[18] The corruption perception index (CPI) is a poll drawn on 17 surveys from 13 independent national and international institutions. CPI ranks countries according to the perception of business people, academic and country analysts of the levels of politicians and public officials' corruption. Countries included were featured in at least three of these surveys. CPI ranges from ten to zero: the least corrupt country (ranked first) receives a score close to ten and the most corrupt (ranked last) receives a score close to zero. For more details, see Lambsdorff (2002) and Transparency International (2006).

[19] India's HDI improved steadily from 0.411 in 1975 to 0.611 in 2004. Adult female literacy rates increased from 36 percent in 1980 to 48 percent in 2004. (Youth female literacy dropped from 54 percent to 68 percent, respectively). Child malnutrition dropped from 71 percent to 53 percent. Primary education completion rate increased from 77.1 percent in 1995 to 88.5 percent in 2004, accompanied with a narrowing of the gender gap between boys' and girls' enrollment (The World Bank 2006 & India). Moreover, the gender parity index (GPI) (a value of unity indicating parity between the sexes) for the gross enrollment rate in secondary education improved from 60 percent in 1991 to 80 percent in 2004 (UNDP, 2006).

schools in India (U.S. DOS, 2006a, Section 6b). In October 2006, the Indian government extended the ban to child domestic labor (under age 14) to include the hospitality sectors, such as child labor in teashops, restaurants, hotels, motels, spas and other recreational centers (Pandey, 2006).

Recent studies indicate the gradual narrowing of education and political representation and participation gaps between different castes, and a narrowing of the gender gap, even though at a slow rate (Krishna, 2003; U.S. DOS, 2007a). Furthermore, the presence and effective roles of non-government organizations (NGOs) in freeing MDS victims, and eradicating modern-day slavery and other forms of discrimination in India, were praised by world leaders in their efforts against MDS practices (U.S. DOS, 2004b; Das Gupta, et al., 2000).

4. Modern-Day Slavery Statistics

Estimates of modern-day slavery vary significantly due to the complexity and illegality of MDS practices. Modern-day slavery is currently considered illegal in almost all countries where governments have signed international and regional agreements and laws regarding the protection of human rights and the elimination of all forms of modern-day slavery. LDC governments often deny the presence of modern-day slavery in their countries, or downplay its extent for fear of losing trade privileges, foreign assistance, foreign investment, or even out of mere national pride.[20] Also, many MDS victims may not recognize their enslavement status since they inherit their 'inferior' status (based on being minority, marginalized or outcast). They may not have the conception that they

---

[20] For example, despite multiple credible reports of existing child bondage in India, government officials say that child bondage is rare. Instead, the government has shifted its focus toward public awareness about child labor (Coursen-Neff, 2003; Human Rights Watch, 2003; ILO, 2005). The definition of *rights* can differ significantly, such that the violations of human rights, including MDS practices, can occur without being identified as violations. Examples of such differences include whether rights belong to individuals or groups; "whether rights are to be considered as side-constraints on goal-promoting actions or, instead as one part of the social goal that is being promoted;" and, "what rights are to be understood as rights *to*" (Nussbaum, 2000, p. 97). Such differences and difficulties in defining *rights* make it equally, or more, difficult to define and identify the violations of *rights*.

have been wronged. Consequently, these victims tend to accept the prevailing norms and practices in their surrounding communities that make them ignorant about the violations of their basic human rights and capabilities (Nussbaum, 2000, p. 140). Even if victims recognize the violation of their rights, the personal shame and stigma associated with being enslaved, may deter many of them from identifying themselves as slaves.

The application of different criteria and procedures by international organizations, NGOs, and governments adds to the difficulty of identifying and counting MDS victims accurately and objectively.[21] The credibility and the motives of organizations or agents that make such estimates may tempt them to overstate or understate the number of MDS victims in LDCs. For instance, the number of child laborers (between the ages of 5 and 14) in India varies, depending on how the terms "labor" and "child labor" are defined. The figures range from 16.4 million, according to the 2004 Indian government's national survey[22], to 44 million (mostly SC/ST), according to the ILO, to 55 million, according to NGOs, to 115 million, according to Human Rights Watch (Anti Slavery International, 2002; ILO, 2001). According to UNICEF, 14 percent of children between the age of 5 and 14 were engaged in labor (U.S. DOS, 2007a, Section 6). According to the Indian government's 2001 reports, more than 266,000 bonded laborers were identified and freed, between 1976 and 2001. In contradiction to the government reports, the Indian Supreme Court, in 1995, commissioned surveys in 13 states (after these states declared that no bonded laborers existed in their jurisdictions). The only published survey, reported over one million bonded laborers in the state of Tamil Nadu alone. The other 12

---

[21] According to a Tamil Nadu government official, many district magistrates in the state (and other states in India) did not understand the definition of bonded labor, and disagreed with it (Human Rights Watch, 2003).

[22] The Indian government's estimate of working children increased from 12.66 million working children in 2001 (U.S. DOS 2007a: Section 6d).

reports have not been published. Previously, in 1978-79, a survey by the Gandhi Peace Foundation and the National Labor Institute estimated 2.617 million bonded laborers (Anti-Slavery International, 1997; Human Rights Watch, 2003; ILO, 2001). The Indian government rejected that estimate because of its methodology and processes of identifying bonded laborers (ILO 2001). Human Rights Watch (1996) estimated the number of bonded laborers in India to be about 15 million. Most studies of child labor (usually using household surveys) miss significant categories of children at risk, such as street children, children engaging in prostitution or bonded labor (Fafchamps and Wahba, 2006, p. 11).

According to the Bonded Labor Liberation Front (BLLF), there are 200,000–300,000 bonded laborers just in the handmade-woolen-carpet industry in India (Jacobs, 1996). Human Rights Watch reported, in 2005, that production of silk thread still depended on bonded children in some states in India (U.S. DOS, 2006a, Section 6).

The percentage of child prostitutes among the 2.3 million prostitutes in India ranges from 15 percent, according to the ILO, to 22 percent, according to NGOs. According to U.N. estimates, 40 percent of all prostitutes were below 18 years of age (U.S. DOS, 2006a, Section 5).

Estimates vary regarding cross-border trafficking of MDS victims. India is considered a source, transit point, and destination for trafficked persons, especially for forced labor and prostitution across borders (U.S. DOS, 2006b). Children are trafficked to other countries in Asia, the Middle East, and the West. Bangladeshi girls and boys are trafficked through India to Pakistan and the Persian Gulf: girls to be exploited as prostitutes or maids, and boys as camel jockeys.[23] The number of trafficked women and children for sex trade from

---

[23] Most of these boys enter the Persian Gulf as dependents of women who already had a visa for the Gulf, and with the knowledge of the children's parents who receive about $200 for their child labor. These children usually end up as beggars in Saudi Arabia during the Hajj (Muslim Holiest) season. MDS perpetrators who bring these children to the Persian Gulf, make about $150 per month from each child labor/enslavement (U.S. DOS, 2003a, Section 6d).

India's neighboring states such as Nepal and Bangladesh into India ranges from 12,000-50,000 annually, including 6,000-10,000 children (U.S. DOS, 2005a, Section 5).

Chapter 2

The Making of a Slave

1. Modern-Day Slavery: A Manifestation of "The Fall"

"Among my people are wicked men who lie in wait like men who snare birds and like those who set traps to catch men. Like cages full of birds, their houses are full of deceit; they have become rich and powerful and have grown fat and sleek. Their evil deeds have no limit; they do not plead the case of the fatherless to win it, they do not defend the rights of the poor. Should I not punish them for this?" declares the Lord. "Should I not avenge myself on such a nation as this?" (Jeremiah 5: 26-29)

The above Biblical verses reveal valuable descriptions of the perpetrators, enslaveables, victims, the process of enslavement, and the enslavement rent (the perpetrators' gain from MDS practices). The perpetrators aim to enrich themselves at the expense of their victims. They act strategically, gathering information about their potential victims (the enslaveables), setting up effective entrapment schemes, and waiting for effective execution to enslave their victims. The verses emphasize that the perpetrators' evil deeds have no limit in their pursuit to entrap and exploit the most vulnerable, marginalized, and weary victims. The perpetrators gain at the expense of inflicting significant pain on their victims. Their lack of regard for the well-being of the victims makes enslavement an integral part of their schemes, as long as it will maximize (or add to) their share of the enslavement rent.

Section 2 identifies the participants in MDS practices and their major attributes. The process of making a slave is highlighted in Section 3, which illustrates the schemes used by the perpetrators to entrap the enslaveables, transform them into MDS victims, and perpetuate MDS practices. Section 4 illustrates the notion of "enslavement rent," and the main social losses/costs of modern-day slavery.

2. The Participants in Modern-Day Slavery Practices

A careful classification of the different participants in MDS practices (potential victims, actual victims, and MDS perpetrators) helps underline their attributes and the state of interdependency among them. Such information plays a crucial role. On one hand, MDS perpetrators exploit it in their pursuit to single-out and trap their victims from the enslaveables' pool, and to sustain MDS practices. On the other hand, this information is crucial for the intervening agents who seek to rescue MDS victims, prosecute the perpetrators, and eradicate MDS practices (discussed in detail in Chapters 4 and 5).

The three primary participants in MDS practices are the enslaveables, MDS victims, and MDS perpetrators. A fourth category includes secondary, national and international, participants who participate, intentionally or unintentionally, actively or passively, either in perpetuating MDS practices or in eradicating them.

2.1 The enslaveables (potential MDS victims)

The enslaveables are the most vulnerable groups to be enslaved and are the victims of many vicious cycles, which intensify and perpetuate their vulnerability and marginalized status. They are typically members of marginalized and outcast groups or tribes who, because of their perceived inferior ethnicity, race, or religion (e.g., the SC/ST under the Hindu caste system in India), find that their membership in such communities serves as a marker for the MDS perpetrators to entrap them and transform them into MDS victims.[24] They are

---

[24] According to the Indian Center for Indigenous and Tribal Peoples (ICITP), more than 40,000 tribal women from Orissa and Bihar were forced into economic and sexual exploitation. In Punjab, persons were sold in an organized trade in weekend bazaars (U.S. DOS, 2003a, Section 6f).

illiterate and misinformed, due in part to their poverty, lack of access to education, and embedded barriers that perpetuate their marginalized status. According to Weiner (1991), deeply embedded informal norms and traditions in India support the existing beliefs that 'excessive' and 'inappropriate' education for the poor would disrupt existing social arrangements. Primary education is not compulsory, and child labor is not considered illegal. With a lack of compulsory education, inadequate schooling facilities, and widespread poverty, children become economic assets to their poor parents who live near or below the subsistence level. Consequently, poor parents cannot afford to buy books and supplies for their children; they also rely on their children to help in the field or at home (Luschinsky, 1966; Weiner, 1991; U.S. DOS, 2007a, Section 5).

The enslaveables are typically more vulnerable to calamities such as natural crises (e.g., typhoons, floods, droughts, earthquakes) that can damage or destroy their primary assets and sources of income (i.e., homes, land, tools, or animals); manmade shocks such as raids, invasions, or other schemes provoked by MDS perpetrators[25]; and personal crises such as sickness, death, or abandonment (by husbands or fathers, the major income earners). Some of the enslaveables are the children of greedy parents, especially where certain embedded traditions and norms support (or do not effectively oppose or prohibit) practices such as selling children for money or accepting slavery-like transactions. There are about a half a million street children in India living in abject poverty, who are mostly orphans or runaways who have been abused, or abandoned by their parents, and become easy targets as MDS victims.[26] Consequently, the

---

[25] According to the Tamil Nadu-based NGO, Legal Resources for Social Actions, raids and violence by Hindu upper castes against SC/ST villages, destroying their possessions and heightening their vulnerability and desperation in the process, have led to more MDS practices such as child bondage (Human Rights Watch, 2003)

[26] These street children are often forced to work 18-20 hour days, frequently in hazardous conditions. They suffer sexual and mental abuses, and are at high risk for sexually transmitted diseases (U.S. DOS, 2003a, Section 5; UNICEF, 2004).

enslaveables are more likely to accept any loan, cash advance, or employment offer.[27]

Studies show that many of the aboriginal tribes (also known as Scheduled Tribes (ST)) in India, who face dire poverty in their marginal lands, are forced to migrate, in search of work. MDS perpetrators exploit the vulnerability of these tribe members and trap them into enslavement (Bulsara and Sreenivasa, 2003-2004). Most of these victims are forced or coerced into the sex trade (U.S. DOS, 2005a, Section 6f). Lastly, most of the enslaveables are members of tribes or marginalized groups who already accept or internalize modern-day slavery as their fate or destiny, a punishment for previous misconduct, or for a better reincarnation, e.g., the SC/ST in India and Buddhist women in Thailand (The Economist, 1996). In summary, the enslaveables are, in part, poor and marginalized by design.

2.1.2 A case study: The Scheduled Castes and Scheduled Tribes (SC/ST): The enslaveables of the Hindu caste system in India

When we are working, they ask us not to come near them. At tea canteens, they have separate tea tumblers and they make us clean them ourselves and make us put the dishes away ourselves. We cannot enter temples. We cannot use upper-caste water taps. We have to go one kilometer away to get water... When we ask for our rights from the government, the municipality officials threaten to fire us. So we don't say anything. This is what happens to people who demand their rights. A Dalit manual scavenger, Ahmedabad district, Gujarat, India (Human Rights Watch, 1999, p. 1)

The caste system in India began about 1500 B.C., after nomadic Aryan tribes invaded and conquered the *Dravidians*, the aboriginal inhabitants of India from around 3000 B.C., as an integral part of the Hindu religion/culture. It is one of the world's longest surviving social

---

[27] In some cases, parents, knowingly, sell their daughters to the sex sector. Female infants, 1-2 years old, were purchased, from their parents, by persons wanting to train them for sex trade and pornography. In Punjab, persons were sold in weekend bazaars (U.S. DOS, 2002a, Section 6f).

hierarchies (Human Rights Watch, 1999, p. 24). The term caste refers to *Jati* (birth group) and *varna* (order, class, or kind). The major castes, from the top down, are the *Brahmans* (priests and spiritual leaders), *Kshatriyas* (rulers and warriors), *Vaishyas* (traders and merchants), and *Shudras* (artisans and servants). Moreover, there are thousands of sub-castes, within these four caste groups.

The Hindu caste system is intrinsically unequal, in that the social, religious, and economic rights for each caste are predetermined by birth, and are hereditary. The primary unit of society in the Hindu social order is caste, not the individual. Accordingly, individual's rights are due to her/his belonging to a particular caste.[28]

The SC/ST, also known as the *Dalits* (literally means broken or depressed), are the descendants of the *Dravidian*. They are positioned at the bottom, below the lowest Hindu caste. They are formerly known as the *Untouchables (or Ati shudras)* because they were considered unclean due to their contact with "blood, death, and dirt." They "must avoid connubial, commensal and many other forms of social contacts with those clusters of patrifamilies who are 'clean'" (Kolenda, 1966, p. 15). "[T]he usual pattern of 'ritual pollution' among castes prevailed... Privileges went to the wealthy and powerful who gave assistance to the poor and lowly, thus tightening the dependence of the latter which in turn preserve and reinforce the position of the former" (Orenstein, 1966, p. 84). *Harijans,* which means 'children of God', was a more polite name, used by Mahatma Gandhi, for the untouchables.

---

[28] For further details regarding the Hindu caste system and Scheduled Castes and Scheduled Tribes (SC/ST) in India, see Bayly (1999), Das (1982), Freeman (1979), Jaffrelot (2003), Mendelsohn and Vicziany (1998), and Thorat (2002).

The SC/ST, therefore, are considered sub-human beings and unworthy of many rights. They are excluded and relegated to separate villages and colonies. They are limited to the most menial and polluting tasks and occupations, such as leatherwork, street sweeping, scavenging public and private latrines, and removing human and animal wastes.[29]

The presence of the Hindu caste system explains, largely, the perpetuation of modern-day slavery in India into the twenty-first century. In a study on the economics of caste in India, George Akerlof (1976, p. 600) highlights the role of indicators in making exchanges: some indicators owe their existence purely to social conventions rather than to economic information in almost all, conventional economic models. As he clearly states, "In the example of caste the behavior of one member of society toward another is predicted by their respective caste status." Because of the SC/ST inferior status, and the subsequent segregation in dwelling, occupation, personal contact, and marriage with members of other castes, SC/ST cannot break religious and social barriers. They are not treated equally, nor do they have access to opportunities available to other Hindu castes. The behavior of the untouchables as a sub-cultural group is easily predicted by other members of society and by visiting anthropologists and sociologists. Akerlof also stresses the importance of recognizing the historical perspective, which attempts to explain the stability (or disappearance) of institutions over a long period of time (p. 609).

---

[29] According to Indian government statistics, about one million SC/ST work as manual scavengers; the majority are women (Anti-Slavery International, 2002). Scavenging is largely a hereditary occupation, and scavengers are typically placed at the very bottom of the cast hierarchy, even the hierarchy of the Dalit sub-castes. The practice of manual scavenging still exists in many states, even though it is outlawed by the Employment of Manual Scavengers and Construction of Dry Latrines (Prohibition) Act, 1993. The Dalits' refusal to do so, however, subjects them to severe physical punishment and social ostracism (Human Rights Watch, 1999, pp. 141-42, and Appendix D; U.S. DOS, 2007a, Section 5).

According to Hinduism, all people are reincarnated *(Samsara)* and, depending on the merits of their actions *(Karma),* have a chance to be reborn into a higher caste if they are obedient to the rules of their caste in their current life on earth. As a result, the SC/ST are pressured to accept their status in this life, in hopes of a better reincarnation. Challenging or rejecting their current social status exposes them to harsh punishment in their current lives, and further demotion in their future lives.

The majority of bonded laborers in India are SC/ST, who are taught to follow their *karma* if they hope to achieve a higher caste in future life. They might be required, by existing customs, to perform tasks for upper caste Hindus without remuneration, and are often prohibited from using the same well water, attending the same temples, or marrying persons from a higher caste. Additionally, they face segregation in housing, roads, and public transportation. Also, in addition to being marginalized with respect to space, the SC/ST were also marginalized with respect to time, permitted to use public streets only during scorching afternoons, for fear that their shadows may touch and pollute the upper castes. In certain places, they were forced to announce their passing through public streets by beating on drums or carrying bells. In the workplace they were denied the use of machinery (advanced capital), and were forced into sanitary sections, or the garbage industry, etc. (Guru, 2004).

Most of the SC/ST live in poor rural India, where social and cultural norms are deeply rooted. This, in turn, heightens the SC/ST's social and economic ostracism and vulnerability. Many are malnourished and lack access to health care, and work in poor conditions (Unni, 2001; U.S. DOS, 2007a, Section5). The *Jajmans* (high caste landowners) in rural regions supplement their power, derived from land ownership, with political power, which is used to coerce the *Kamins* (the landless low castes and untouchables). The village *panachayats* (councils), law courts, and police favor the *Jajmans* in disputes with the *Kamins* (Kolenda, 1966, pp. 18-19). This may explain the continuation of exclusive behaviors and the imposition of certain menial and 'unclean' tasks and jobs, such as scavenging, on the lowest castes and the untouchables and the scheduled castes.

In 1935, the British government— in an attempt to offset the effect of a rigid, exclusive, and discriminating caste system— listed the Dalits and other low castes (also known as Backward Castes[30]) in India as Scheduled Castes (SC) to increase their representation in legislature, government, and educational institutions. Likewise, other *Adivasis* (aboriginal) communities – those who rejected the Hindu caste system, resided in forests and mountains, and endured discrimination — were listed as Scheduled Tribes (ST). The emancipation of slavery by the British and the subsequent abolition of the caste system by the Indian government had little effect on changing the economic and social situation of the SC/ST, who continue to be regarded as 'untouchables' (Luke and Munshi, 2004). According to the Census of India (2001), the SC/ST population of 251 million constitutes 24.4 percent of India's population (SC population was 166.6 million, representing 16.2 percent of the total population, and the ST population was 84.4 million, 8.2 percent of the total population).

The Indian Constitution of 1947-48, followed by other acts and laws, outlawed almost all forms of discrimination.[31] The Directive

---

[30] Backward castes (also known as other backward classes) "are those whose ritual ranks and occupational status are above "untouchables" but who themselves remain socially and economically depressed" (Human Rights Watch, 1999, p. 37).

[31] The practice of untouchability that discriminates against SC/ST was abolished by the Protection of Civil Rights Act, 1955. However, recent reports by the Asian Centre for Human

Principles of the Indian Constitution states that the government will promote the education and economic interest of the SC/ST, in addition to protecting them from social injustice and all forms of discrimination.[32] This legislation notwithstanding, discrimination and atrocities against the SC/ST still exist, mainly in the rural areas (Goonesekere, 2001; Human Rights Watch 1999, 2005). This may explain, in part, the government's ongoing acts against specific discriminations.[33] Recent studies show that 50 years after the Constitution, inter-caste disparity between the SC/ST and the rest of India's population still exists, underlying the overall disparity (Deshpande, 2000). Recent reports show that the crime rate against SC/ST has increased by 25 percent since 1991, especially against women, and that many village populations have been wiped out (United Nations, 2000; Thorat, 2002). Between 1981 and 1997, about 200,000 atrocity cases were reported to the authorities. The average number of registered cases of discrimination and atrocities against the SC/ST, after peaking to 3,875 in the 1980s, decreased gradually to 1,157 in 1997.

Recent NGOs' and government reports illustrated how the upper-caste fishing communities discriminated against SC/ST communities after the Tsunami of December 2004, and prevented them from receiving aid. The SC/ST were denied the government-supplied aid and were left homeless. Following the dissemination of these reports of discrimination,

---

Rights show that the untouchability is still widespread, especially in villages and rural regions. For example the SC/ST were not allowed to have access to public places such as community water wells and temples (Chakma, 2007).

[32] According to Gary Haugen (1999), "Injustice occurs when power is misused to take from others what God has given them, namely, their life, dignity, liberty or the fruit of their love and labor." (p. 73)

[33] Examples of such acts are the Protection of Human Rights Act, 1993, the Protection of Civil Rights Act, 1995, and the Scheduled Castes and Scheduled Tribes (Preventions of Atrocities)

28

the government supplied said aid for the SC/ST communities (U.S. DOS, 2006a, Section 5).

In 1993-94, almost one-half of the SC/ST lived below the poverty line, compared to one-third of the rest of population (Thorat, 2002; Overdorf, 2003), which clearly demonstrates the high degree of vulnerability among the SC/ST. According to government data, more than 86 percent of bonded laborers are SC/ST. Recent studies show this percentage to be about 90 percent (Anti-Slavery International, 2003), and that the SC/ST's per capita income is about two-third of other Indians. Adult SC/ST male education is 70 percent, and adult SC/ST female education is about 50 percent, which illustrates the further gender discrimination against SC/ST women (Unni, 2001; Human Rights Watch, 2005).

Continuing government intervention, through affirmative-action programs and reservation quotas (in government employment, higher education, federal government jobs, state legislatures, and educational institutions)[34] to correct market and cultural discriminations against the SC/ST, have made state/public employment for the SC/ST the primary requirement to level the playing field and give access to SC/ST, in terms of public jobs, public service, and political representation (Human Rights Watch, 1999; Guru, 2004).[35]

Act, 1989, and other state and central government laws, in addition to national commissions such as the National Commission for Scheduled Castes and Scheduled Tribes.

[34] The implementation of reservation quota, in some states (e.g., Bihar), has favored the backward castes to the SC/STs, resulting in improving the status of the backward castes relative to the SC/STs (Human Rights Watch, 1999, p. 44). In addition, widespread government corruption obstructs the implementation of affirmative action programs in some other states (Chakma, 2007).

[35] However, the government also uses affirmative-action programs as a deterrent against Dalits who convert to other religions, such as Buddhism, Christianity, or Islam (to avoid discrimination under the caste system), by denying them the benefits of such programs; a typical example of a Catch 22 (Human Rights Watch, 1999).

Even though untouchability (the imposition of social disabilities on SC/ST or Dalits) still exists in the twenty-first century (especially in rural regions in India), studies show that there are signs that untouchability is gradually dissipating in some regions. In those areas, members of higher castes will enter the untouchables' houses, participate in sporting matches with the untouchables, and even share the same temple with untouchables – which were rarely done in the early decades of the twentieth century. However, others signs of untouchability are still held: for example, most women still avoid contact with the untouchables, and the untouchables still keep a distance between themselves and others in some Hindu temples (Orenstein, 1966, p. 86; Human Rights Watch, 1999).

Abraham and Platteau (2001, p. 14) illustrate the vulnerability of the enslaveables in segregated communities: "In these encounters, the elite provides an authority structure which imposes its rule or its interpretation of the traditions on the lower people who have no choice but to comply." The enslaveables do not dare violate or voice their possible disagreement with existing social norms because of their fear of retribution (Elster, 1989, p. 100).[36] The elite groups (e.g., upper castes, public servants, and MDS perpetrators) use their power and privilege to appropriate, deflect, or misuse resources belonging to the vulnerable members of their communities. Meanwhile the enslaveable are entrapped in these communities. The enslaveables perform what is in accordance with a priori social rules defining their social identity (Platteau, 1994a, p. 538). Lastly, the presence of discriminating informal metanorms against certain population groups (e.g., SC/ST in India) deepens the perpetuation of such discriminating norms, according to which one must punish not only the defectors (violators of such norms) but also

---

[36] Social norms are enforced by members of the general community, and not always out of self-interest. Violators of these norms can be subject to severe punishments. There are other types of norms, such as moral norms, legal norms and private norms (Elster, 1989, p. 100).

those who do not punish the defectors (Elster, 1989, p. 109).[37] This explains the chronic poverty in the enslaveables' communities (in contrast to people in transitory poverty). In such communities, the ultra poor are more likely to stay poor for extended periods; they are stuck because they cannot leverage anti-poverty programs (Barrett and Swallow, 2006, p. 2).

The presence of metanorms makes it more difficult for minority groups (such as the SC/ST in India) to oppose these discriminating metanorms because of their fear of collective punishment, in addition to their fear of MDS perpetrators' punishments.[38] Caste recognition (including the separate SC/ST) serves to identify different caste members. Studies show that when trade or transactions take place with strangers (or different groups), the exchanges are often equated to stealing or cheating. Cheating a foreigner (e.g., low caste member or outcast) may even bring social prestige to the individual (Platteau, 1994a, p. 552).

The segregated enslaveables suffer also because of their exclusion and physical and psychological segregation, due to the limited-group morality, restricted to the elite and upper caste groups, and, by definition, not extended to the enslaveables.[39]

Since some population groups (e.g., the enslaveables) in certain societies do not participate – or, more accurately, are not invited to participate (and in extreme cases, are banned from participation) – in the initiation of social norms, the members of these groups are forced to abide by these 'external' norms,

---

[37] For further analysis on metanorms, see Axelrod (1986) and Elster (1989). For details on the effects of metanorms on SC/ST in India, see Akerlof (1976) and Basu (1986). For examples of collective punishments against SC/ST, See Chakma (2007)

[38] Human Rights Watch (2005) reports cases of collective punishments by the higher-caste against Dalits who challenge the social order, in addition to collective punishment by higher castes and higher-caste communities against Dalit villages for individual 'transgressions.' Such punishments, against the poor Dalits who live at or below the subsistence level, may push them close to destitution and starvation. Violence against women and mass rapes by upper-caste gangs are used to intimidate SC/ST and backward castes (U.S. DOS, 2006a, Section 5).

[39] See Platteau (1994b) and Granovetter (1985) for further analysis on norms, types of norms, the costs and rewards of norms, and the use of norms as social capital.

imposed by the more dominant groups in their community or society. The vulnerable groups, such as the enslaveables, are punished when they violate these 'imposed' norms.

The above analysis illustrates that the enslaveables' submissiveness to the control and dominance of caste members, especially the upper castes, relegates the enslaveables to substandard living. The enslaveables, who struggle for survival, cannot invest or entertain other possibilities or capabilities, due to their fear of harsh collective sanctions, a fear supported by credible threats and records. Such sanctions include illegitimate force by MDS perpetrators, used directly to punish MDS victims and the enslaveables, hiring of thugs, and the bribing of police officers, judges, and other public servants, to intervene in their favor. However, MDS perpetrators' actual use of force is not required; implicit or explicit threats are sufficient (Fafchamps, 2004, p. 24)

2.2 MDS victims (or the enslaved)

This category refers to the victimized or enslaved among the enslaveables. They are mostly women and children, who are the least likely to resist, fight back, or even comprehend their status as MDS victims. Their unique attributes (actual and potential) fit the perpetrators' need for designated MDS industries, for example, children's small fingers and tender touch in industries such as hand-kitting carpets and scarves, match boxes, and rolling *beedi* cigarettes, and women and children in forced prostitution, pornography, and pedophilia. Passive and forced, they are subjected to cruel treatments, where they may be locked-up, or even shackled in sweatshops, and face harsh punishment if they fail to deliver the 'excessive' quotas imposed on them by the perpetrators (e.g., rolling *beedi* cigarettes, making and filling matchboxes, or serving customers in brothels). They tend to be voiceless because they fail to receive help or proper intervention when they complain; they are threatened, beaten, burned, or killed. SC/ST children comprise the majority of MDS victims sold into bondage, to pay off debts to MDS perpetrators who are mostly upper-caste creditors (Human Rights Watch, 1999, p. 2). These victims are entrapped into long-term relations, without or with very insignificant negotiating power, skills, or capabilities.

The following five personal cases help illustrate the common attributes of MDS victims.

Debt bondage slavery: Karmela and Sumitbonu, young sisters from the State of Tamil Nadu, had been bonded to the village moneylender for two years because of their parents' debt. They work 10 hours a day, six days a week, each rolling a quota of 1000 *beedis* (hand-rolled cigarettes) a day. Their quotas are delivered to the moneylender, a subcontractor who provides the finished *beedis* to the *Mangalore Ganesh Beedi Works*, an Indian company that bundles and exports *beedis*. Ironically, the bundling process includes wrapping a portion of the output with the U.S. Surgeon General's health warning, which is required before exporting *beedis* to the U.S. markets. As usual, the moneylender and company claim that they only employ adult workers and never use bonded or indentured laborers. The moneylender, who essentially owns the two sisters, denies the bonded labor practice, and claims that any debt is usually paid in three or four months. However, a report by the U.S. television show, *60 Minutes*, shows the girls delivering their daily quota of *beedis* later on. Soon after seeing the footage of this televised report, the U.S. Customs Service banned the importation of *beedis* by *Mangalore Ganesh*, and an Indian court heard the cases of the sisters and others. Consequently, they have been granted their freedom (CBS News, 2000).

Forced child prostitution: Sumita, a young girl whose mother died when she was eleven, ran away at age 12 after her father wanted to arrange her marriage because he could not care for her. The person who promised to find her a job and housing sold her to a brothel for about $750. She was ordered to serve customers, in order to pay back the loan. She was exposed to physical and emotional abuse for several days before she served her first customer. She defended herself until she realized there was no way out. "You feel like a bird with broken wings," Sumita said. "You don't fly anymore." (Zoba, 1999, p. 37)

Chattel slavery (domestic trafficking): Santosh, a 5-year-old male child was kidnapped while playing with friends in his village in Bahar. He and his friends were driven to Allahabad, the center of India's "Carpet belt," and sold into slavery. No exchange took place (except the exchange between the kidnappers, or slave-traders, and slave-masters who buy the slaves, in case they are separate groups). Santosh was forced to work 12-19 hours a day for nine years. He was locked in a room with no direct light or proper ventilation, and worked with no breaks. He experienced vision damage, lung disease, and injuries from sharp tools. He never received any monetary payment; he was given only enough food to keep him alive. After being rescued, he had practically no emotion left in him (Jacobs, 1996).

Inherited slavery: Ramon was born into slavery to low-caste parents. He, his father, and his grandfather had worked for the same brick kiln to pay back an advanced payment paid by the brick kiln manager to Ramon's grandfather. Ramon and his family earn the equivalent of US 2 cents per 80-kilogram bag of brick. They represent a typical case of debt-bondage. Their owner inflicts physical punishment when they fail to work hard and submit the required quota; and, the owner's threats of hunting them down and bribing police to arrest them prevent them from escaping or reporting their MDS status (U.S. DOS, 2006a).

International slave trafficking: Reena, a twelve-year-old from Nepal, was brought to India by her aunt, who sold her to a brothel owner in New Delhi. She was forced to have sex with many clients every day. She was trapped in the brothel since she did not speak Hindu and because she was afraid of the police: Reena had seen police officers collect money from the brothel owners for every new girl brought in. She was told to say that she was 25 years old and had joined the brothel voluntarily. Reena escaped after two years, and has devoted her life to helping other trafficking victims escape (U.S. DOS, 2006b, Section I).

2.3 MDS primary perpetrators

In his arrogance the wicked man hunts down the weak, who are caught in the schemes he devises. (Psalms 10:2)

If you see the poor oppressed in a district, and justice and rights denied, do not be surprised at such things. (Ecclesiastes 4:3)

MDS perpetrators plan and prepare to hunt down their victims. They continuously invest in skills, knowledge regarding their potential victims (the enslaveables), and possible interventions and intervening agents against MDS practices. They take advantage of their victims' vulnerability and neediness. The two major categories of perpetrators are the recruiters (or traders) and the eventual MDS perpetrators.

The perpetrators, acting similar to typical economic agents, seek to maximize their share of the potential stream of net income (enslavement rent) from MDS industries. They continually invest not only to maximize their gain and survive competition in regular markets where all participants (e.g., owners, workers, and buyers) can potentially win, but also to maximize their share in the enslavement rent. They gain at the expense of larger loss to the victims (e.g., indentured laborers, forced prostitutes, sweatshop workers), by extracting value from these victims without compensation. Accordingly, MDS perpetrators are primarily rent seekers who invest in schemes to sustain their share in the enslavement rent and to avoid prosecution.[40] Thus, MDS perpetrators target and

---

[40] Rent seeking simply refers to the behavior of one party (the rent seeker) to increase its share of the pie, without increasing the size of the pie; thus, lowering the share of others, and gaining at the expense of others. Rent seekers collect rents on capital they do not own. Therefore, their gain must be at the expense of the owners of such capital. Examples of rent-seeking behaviors include monopolists who raise the price of their products and gain at the expense of the buyers of their products; domestic producers who seek trade protection (such as import quota and tariffs) to enable them to raise their price domestically and gain market share at the expense of foreign exporters and domestic buyers; and, a typical example of rent seeking that takes place

manipulate their potential victims, the enslaveables, in MDS schemes (e.g., cash advance, debt-bondage, promises of employment and marriage schemes, outright kidnapping of victims). Thereafter, MDS perpetrators transform the potential victims into MDS victims. Then, they entrap and coerce these victims to participate in MDS practices. These stages of making a slave are explained later in this chapter.

Consequently, MDS perpetrators align their efforts and schemes to take advantage of existing institutional frameworks to sustain their MDS practices and their share of the enslavement rent. They are active participants and self-calculating agents with well-defined plans to gain from the vulnerability of the enslaveables and the existing institutional framework. They generally take advantage of complex sets of informal traditions and ideologies and formal rules to target and entrap the most vulnerable victims. They reduce their search cost by concentrating their search in the enslaveables' communities, in very/ultra poor areas/regions, exploiting any institutional bias/discrimination against these communities. Moreover, they collaborate with interest groups and corrupt officials, especially at the local levels, to make it difficult to penetrate MDS markets, prosecute MDS perpetrators, or eradicate MDS practices.

2.4 Secondary/external participants

> Woe to those who make unjust laws, to those who issue oppressive decrees, to deprive the poor of their rights and withhold justice from the oppressed of my people, making widows their prey and robbing the fatherless. (Isaiah 10:1-2)

Domestic participants, including local, state, and national public servants, can take different sides in MDS practices. On one side, the list includes corrupt politicians, police officers, judges, and other officials who, typically, do not

---

outside regular markets is theft, where the thieves' gain is made possible at the expense of their victims.

initiate the enslavement process, but may collaborate with MDS perpetrators, seeking a share of the enslavement rent. The public-choice theory (Buchanan, 2003) explains the inclination of these officials to look after their own personal interest, receiving bribes or a share of the enslavement rent, in the case of modern-day slavery, instead of prosecuting MDS perpetrators and serving the interest of MDS victims and the enslaveables. On the other side, other officials, government agencies, and NGOs intervene against MDS practices, defending the interests of the enslaveables and MDS victims.

International participants include multinational corporations, importing companies, tourists, international organizations, foreign and international non-governmental organizations (NGOs), and consumers (this group also includes similar domestic participants). Their participation may take one of the following forms:

1. Active and direct participants, such as owners of overseas brothels and participants in slave trafficking, in addition to foreign consumers of MDS products, such as pedophiles, sex tourists, and pornographers.[41]

2. Active and indirect participants, such as importers and multinational corporations who seek cheaper inputs to compete against aggressive competition and enlarge their profit margin, or market share.

3. Passive or unintended participants, such as importers and multinational corporations, which trade in slave-produced goods because of their lower cost, or because of the flexibility and the informal practice of such business. This group also includes consumers, or ultimate users,

---

[41] There are more than one million children exploited in the global commercial sex trade. Sex tourists from foreign countries usually travel to LDCs, seeking anonymity and the availability of children in prostitution. By doing so, these child sex tourists avoid prosecution in their own countries, taking advantage of the lack of, or ineffective, law enforcement against MDS industries such as forced prostitution and pedophilia, accompanied with widespread corruption in these LDCs (U.S. DOS, 2006b, Section I).

who buy slave-produced goods because of their lower prices or unique attributes, not knowing the role of slavery in production).

4. Active anti-MDS practices such as slave-abolitionist consumers and firms, and foreign and international NGOs, which deliberately act to eradicate MDS practices around the world, such as the American Anti-Slavery Group, Amnesty International, Anti-Slavery International, Free the Slaves, Human Rights Watch (HRW), and International Justice Mission (IJM).

5. International organizations such as the International Labor Organization (ILO), United Nations, UNICEF, and the World Bank, which aim to protect human rights, and develop poor and marginalized communities in LDCs.

3. The Enslavement Process

The enslavement transformation process usually occurs in three stages: First, the entrapping of the enslaveables; second, transforming the enslaveables into MDS victims; and third, the perpetuation of MDS practices.

3.1 First stage: Entrapping the enslaveables

The recruitment/entrapment of MDS victims usually involves one of the following arrangements: cash advance/debt, false promises (education, employment, or marriage) or outright kidnapping.

Cash-advance or debt bondage: Offered by MDS recruiters and perpetrators to desperate enslaveables, these practices serve as immediate relief. Due to the lack of collateral owned by the enslaveables, the perpetrators target certain members of the enslaveables' families, such as women and children, as collateral (to be exploited in MDS industries), until the 'debt' is fully paid. The victims and their families are typically unaware of the terms of the debt or cash advance; they are least likely to be able to pay such undefined debt (which includes inflated interest payments, other overstated costs associated with late payment, failure to pay on time, etc). The vulnerability of the enslaveables increases with the level of devastating shocks to which they are exposed. Such shocks include the loss of their assets due to natural, economic, or manmade crises, personal shocks such as death or sickness, and cultural and social obligations such as excessive dowry payments by brides' parents, and their immediate need for help. Consequently, the enslaveables cannot afford the luxury of thinking about the potential harms and abuse of such cash advance and debt offers, because of their dire situation. The enslaveables' desperation and the significant information gap between them and the MDS perpetrators serve to boost the perpetrators' enslavement rent.

False-promise schemes: Schemes such as lucrative employment, education, or marriage offers to women and children, usually from other parts of the country or abroad, are commonly used by MDS recruiters in poor and marginalized areas.[42] These recruiters, equipped with 'apparently legal' documentations and representations, depend on the enslaveables' inferior information and illiteracy to trick them into signing, or accepting such contracts, which eventually will entrap them into becoming MDS victims. Subsequently, the victims are usually transported (or trafficked) to a different region in the same country or to a foreign country, where they are sold and forced to work in sweatshops or brothels. The enslaveable families are more likely to fall into these false promise schemes because of their desperate and vulnerable status, lack of more legitimate offers, and because these false offers are too lucrative to reject. Dire poverty, lack of viable alternatives, and the low social status of the enslaveables, especially females, contribute to the success of these schemes, so that parents accept these schemes/offers from strangers (MDS perpetrators),

---

[42] For example, young girls and boys between the ages of 12 and 18 from the rural area of Andhra Pradesh, India, were recruited to work in U.S.-based restaurants and apartment businesses. Upon arrival, they were put to work in a prostitution ring (U.S. DOS, 2000a, Section 6f).

promising employment for their children, or marriage for their daughters. In some cases, the parents receive payment or the promise of payment to be sent by their children. Once these victims are trafficked from poverty-stricken regions/states to other richer regions/states, they are forced into prostitution or other forms of MDS practices, according to NGO reports (U.S. DOS, 2005a, Section 5).

In the above two cases, MDS recruiters/perpetrators utilize their information to recruit their victims according to the victims' specific vulnerability, such as their desperate need for instant cash for funeral, medical expenses, 'dowry' expenses, loss of assets or employment. The false promise offers are usually accompanied by cash-advances, to lure the enslaveables' families to accept such offers. MDS recruiters/perpetrators, supported by professional, and seemingly credible, representations, add enough legitimacy to recruit potential victims. The advanced payment is usually used to speed up the enslavement process.

Outright kidnappings: Outright kidnappings occur frequently, most often in the case of orphans and abandoned street children. MDS perpetrators exploit the fact that many children do not have birth certificates, personal registration or identification, which makes it difficult for their families to report a missing child. The fear of prosecution (because of their failure to register their children) deters the families of the kidnapped children from reporting such incidents.[43] Other children are kidnapped and trafficked overseas, for example, the case of child prostitution and camel jockeys in the Persian Gulf states.[44]

---

[43] Child laborers were sold in an organized ring at the annual Sonepur cattle fair in Bihar, India, as recently as December 1999. Victims were the children of impoverished families in surrounding areas, brought to the fair and sold for the purposes of domestic labor and forced sexual services (U.S. DOS, 2000a, Section 6c).

[44] Boys, as young as age four, are being trafficked there. Between 100 and 1000 underage South Asian camel jockeys are currently working in the United Arab Emirates alone. Most of these children were sent with the knowledge of their parents, who receive up to $200; the rest were kidnapped. The gang bringing the jockeys earns approximately $150 per month from the labor of each child. The children's names are added to the passport of Indian or Bangladeshi women, who

MDS perpetrators typically provide the efficient level of quality for the salient attributes that are desired by the enslaveables. Instant cash advances, employment offers, promises of steady income, and provision of credit are offered to desperate enslaveables, who are very vulnerable to making hurried decisions and accept these offers, because of their dire situation and lack of viable options. The enslaveables become victim of bounded rationality, because their rational choices are limited by their passion (or emotional affect), stupidity (or cognitive ability) and ignorance (or imperfect information) (Kaufman, 2007). In addition, the enslaveables become victims of the MDS perpetrators' manipulation of offers not accompanied by lengthy formal contracts, collateral requirements, or even the official identification of the enslaveables. What the enslaveables do not know is the other non-salient attributes of these offers or transactions that lead to their entrapment and transformation into victims of MDS practices. The perpetrator strategically shares the salient attributes that correspond to the immediate needs of the desperate enslaveables, concealing the enslavement attributes, which usually take place only after the first phase of the transactions (e.g., the cash delivery, the transportation of the 'potential victims'). Meanwhile, the enslaveables are typically caught in these take-it-or-leave-it offers, which they cannot afford to reject, given their desperation and bounded rationality.[45]

3.2 Second stage: Transforming the enslaveables into MDS victims

The process of transforming the recruited/kidnapped victims usually involves one or more of the following schemes. One entails imposing excessive daily quotas on MDS victims, such as a minimum quota of *beedis* or hand knitted carpets/scarves, and a minimum number of customers served in brothels. The

---

already have visas for the Gulf States, as their children. Trafficked girls and women end up as domestic workers or sex workers (U.S. DOS, 2005a, Section 5).

[45] For further analysis of bounded rationality and the salience of offer attributes, see Korobkin (2003).

failure to produce or supply such quotas is deterred by harsh punishment schemes that range from regular detention, beating, burning, sinking heads under water, and inflicting permanent physical harm, to killing. The punishment serves to intimidate the victims and quell them into submission; the harsher the punishment, the more apprehensive the victims, and the more likely that they will produce or supply the 'excessive' quota according to the perpetrators' specification. Extreme punishments are used primarily in extreme cases, for example, when victims try to escape or report MDS practices to the police or media, or to affirm the perpetrators' credible threats.[46] The quota system may also be imposed on MDS victims who work at home, with the perpetrators exploiting their own reputation of inflicting serious harm on non-cooperating victims or their families in order to force the victims to supply the excessive quota according to the perpetrators' specification.[47] The victims in this case may receive help from other family members, in order to supply their quota on time. If the victims fail to submit their assigned quota, they may be taken away, sold to other perpetrators, transported to other regions where the victims lose all family support, or locked-up in a perpetrator's sweatshop.

Another scheme involves the trafficking of victims to other regions in the country (domestic or internal trafficking) or to foreign countries (international trafficking) and selling them to other recruiters or to the ultimate MDS perpetrators, where the victims are usually given new identities. Confiscating the victims' personal identification and imposing false identification, especially in

---

[46] A Tamil Nadu, India-based NGO reported that violence by perpetrators against MDS victims, and by upper social castes against the enslaveables (SC/ST) is directly linked to a rise in MDS practices. Violence against the SC/ST usually follows any complaints or political activism by SC/ST (Human Rights Watch, 2003).

[47] The relationship between the MDS victims and MDS perpetrators typically follows the reputation-based exchange instead of trust-based exchange. Due to the involuntary participation of MDS victims, MDS perpetrators exploit their reputation of using excessive punishment as the mechanism to ensure the implementation of their MDS practices and schemes.

slave trafficking within the country or internationally, severs the relation between the victims and their families. The perpetrators may use false documents that claim the MDS victims as their relatives (e.g., daughters, sons, or wives) to facilitate the trafficking of MDS victims. India is ranked in Tier 2 Watch List, according to the U.S. Department of State's annual Trafficking in Person Reports, and is classified as a source, transit, and destination of forced and bonded labor and commercial sexual exploitation (U.S. DOS, 2006b, Section VI).[48]

A third scheme may involve the victims in criminal activities (e.g., prostitution, drug peddling), or falsely make them believe that they are sought-after criminals, convincing the victims to obey the perpetrators' orders of excessive quotas. The victims' fear of collaboration between the perpetrators and the authorities nudges them closer to MDS victim status.

The above schemes make the most of an MDS victim's unwillingness to report MDS practices, for fear of retaliation by MDS perpetrators. There is also the hesitation to identify themselves as victims, upon contact with law enforcement authorities, because of their fear of real or imagined retaliation by MDS perpetrators or by law enforcement officers, who may be in collaboration with MDS perpetrators (U.S. DOS, 2006b, Section I; Chakma, 2007).

3.3 Third stage: Perpetuating modern-day slavery practices

---

[48] The U.S. DOS Trafficking in Persons Reports (2000b to 2006b) rank countries in three tiers: Tier 1 includes countries that fully comply with the minimum standards of the Trafficking Victims Protection Act (TVPA) of 2000. Tier 2 includes countries whose governments do not fully comply with the minimum standards of TVPA: however, they are making significant effort toward complying with such standards. Tier 3 includes countries whose governments fail to comply with the minimum standards and are not making significant effort to do so. Tier 2 of the Watch List includes countries, such as India, with, first, significant absolute numbers or a significant increase in the numbers of victims of severe forms of trafficking; second, failure to provide evidence of increasing effort to combat severe forms of trafficking in the previous year; and, third, determination that the country is making significant effort to improve its compliance above the minimum standards over the next year (U.S. DOS, 2006b, Section I).

MDS practices will continue to exist, so long as they are rewarding enough to incite perpetrators to expand or sustain such practices. The process of perpetuating modern-day slavery reflects or mirrors the process of perpetuating the enslavement rent. The following analysis illustrates the major factors that contribute to the perpetuation of modern-day slavery, which, in turn, sustains the stream of enslavement rent.

3.3.1 The perpetrators' role in perpetuating modern-day slavery: MDS perpetrators seek to carry on MDS practices through perpetuating the outstanding debt owed by MDS victims or their families. Such a tactic may take one or more of the following forms: charging a very high interest rate, as high as 200 percent or more annually, on loans to MDS victims' families. Low wages (or pecuniary compensation), high interest rates, and escalating the victims' outstanding debt make it impossible for the victims (or their families) to pay the debt (The Economist, 1996). Since the perpetrators are the holders of the debt accounts, they can manipulate them to their advantage. The debt is the legal record used by the perpetrators in response to any legal inquiry or concerns of the victims' families. The perpetrators can also enlarge the victims' costs (spent on such items as the victims' food, clothes, shelter, and other financial penalties related to work) so that they exceed the value of the victims' labor. Therefore, the outstanding debt may increase, instead of decreasing over time. The perpetrators also exploit the MDS victims' (and their families') ignorance regarding the outstanding debt. In addition, the victims and their families are typically too weary and overwhelmed to worry about the outstanding debt. Second, MDS perpetrators make explicit credible threats against MDS victims and their families, to intimidate the victims and sustain their submission and obedience.[49] Third, they usually entrap MDS victims in criminal activities, and/or change their personal identification, with the result that MDS victims become sought-after 'criminals'. Consequently, the victims are less likely to escape or report MDS practices to the authorities. Fourth, the perpetrators sustain sophisticated collaboration with government agents (e.g., corrupt politicians, judges, and police officers) through bribes or shares in the enslavement rent.[50]

3.3.2 The victims' passive role in perpetuating modern-day slavery: The victims' despair, fear, and overwhelming physical and mental constraints, such as shackles, lock-in brothels or sweatshops, branding, and the threat of harming or enslaving victims' relatives are among the major factors in the victims' passive role in perpetuating enslavement. Victims fear the perpetrators' harsh punishment, and are less likely to report MDS practices to authorities if they fear being prosecuted. This is especially true if the victims are entrapped in illegal activities by the perpetrators, for example, withholding of victims' personal documents, forging the personal identification of the victims, and forcing the victims to participate in illegal activities such as prostitution.[51] The victims may also be deceived into believing that they are criminals, and are being chased by the police or other legal authorities. Even though such fear is unfounded, it plays a very important role in dimming the victims' outlook and expectations and makes them more inclined to accept their enslavement status. The victims' fear deepens in the case of actual or perceived corrupt authorities, where police officers and other

---

[49] Explicit credible threats in MDS practices differ from the ones concealed/implicit in normal transactions behind the screen of mutual goodwill (Platteau, 1944a, p. 546).

[50] The National Commission for Women in India (NCW) reported that organized crime subjected women and children to extortion, beating, and rape, with the help of police corruption and collusion (U.S. DOS, 2005a, Section 5).

[51] Despite the intended objectives of helping MDS victims in India, NGO studies warned of the built-in ambiguity in the laws, which, although intended to protect trafficking victims, has been exploited to protect the sex industry. Eighty to ninety percent of the arrests made in the West Bengal state in the 1990's, under the Immoral Trafficking and Prevention Act (ITPA) of 1986, were of female sex workers, rather than traffickers, pimps, or other secondary participants, as it was intended. Only a small fraction of arrests made involved the traffickers (U.S. DOS, 2000a and 2003a, Section 6f).

officials collaborate with the MDS perpetrators, or even act as MDS perpetrators for a larger share of the enslavement rent.[52]

The victims' fear and distrust of life after slavery may induce them to accept (or not reject) their enslavement as their destiny. Some victims may be too afraid to start again, since they were tricked, enslaved, and punished when they tried to escape or complain. Their acceptance of MDS practices reflects their loss of hope, and their lack of faith that society may free them or interfere on their behalf. In extreme cases, the victims may fear freedom itself. This idea is clearly stated by a former slave: "I could not understand what freedom meant" (Wright, 1993, p. 2). Freedom may mean loss of what the victims already have, regardless of how oppressive and cruel. They may fear abandonment, or worse treatment, if they are caught and sold again. This reflects the victims' distrust in community support or intervention, and their fear of excessive retaliation by the perpetrators, which, in a twisted way, makes the acceptance of modern-day slavery a 'safe' or 'secure' option; the lesser of two evils.

3.3.3 Economic factors: The major economic factor in the perpetuation of MDS practices is the prevalence of dire poverty (or ultra poverty), especially in the marginalized communities. In 1993-94, nearly one-half of the SC/ST lived below the poverty line, compared to one third of the rest of the population (Thorat, 2002). Extreme poverty tends to concentrate in slums, shantytowns, and marginalized rural areas, where the poor live, who lack the basic needs such as food, health, education, water and sanitation, and shelter. Poor and marginalized regions typically lack basic physical infrastructure such as clean water, sanitation, electricity, and roads, and social infrastructure such as primary schools, adult training and employment centers, health clinics, and credit facilities. The lack of these infrastructures, in the areas where most of the vulnerable SC/ST in India

---

[52] Reports show that prison officials and officers used female prisoners as domestic servants, and sold them to brothels (U.S. DOS, 2003a, Section 6f).

live, intensifies the vulnerability of the enslaveables. Lack of effective
government anti-poverty policies and adequate safety nets during crises tends to
heighten the enslaveables' vulnerability. Economic dualism, in terms of the
skewed distribution of government spending and development programs,
explains, in part, the sustained vulnerability of the enslaveables.

The Dalits in rural India, typically, are agrarian workers for caste
landowners, are paid in kind (usually rice), or labor for very low wages, below the
subsistence level (less than one dollar per day). They are also obligated to perform
certain tasks, without pay or with very little compensation, such as scavenging,
digging graves, disposal of dead animals, and cleaning of human waste. They lack
access to all forms of capital, such as physical capital (e.g., machines, equipment,
structures, land), social capital (e.g., social networks), human capital (education
and health), and financial capital (e.g., cash, credit). In addition, the Dalits, in
their poor communities, typically lack access to physical public capital (e.g., clean
water, sanitation, and electricity) and social public capital, such as health services
(clinics and hospitals), financial services (credit and lending facilities),
educational services (such as public schools and adult education services),
security services (e.g., police and fire departments/stations), and legal services
(e.g., public administration offices and courts).

3.3.4 Legal and governance factors: These factors reflect the absence of
laws against modern-day slavery, loopholes in existing laws, lack of effective
enforcement of existing laws that protect the enslaveables' interests and human
rights, and the level of embedded corruption in the legal system.[53] The victims'
lack of effective access to the legal system is likely to sustain MDS practices.

---

[53] Credible human rights' monitors in India report that some state commissions have not
yet demonstrated effective, independent protection of human rights. Other reports show that the
government prohibited child forced and bonded labor, yet, did not enforce such prohibitions
effectively, especially in the informal sector (U.S. DOS, 2003a, Section 4 and 6d). In addition,
according to the ILO (2003), state governments were reluctant to participate in identifying and
releasing child laborers in India.

Victims may fear adverse treatment (due to police corruption and retaliation by MDS perpetrators), may be unable to file legal claims or complaints due to their poverty, and may be unaware of the existence of a legal system and procedures to file complaints (due to their illiteracy and ignorance). The lack of legal centers in poor rural areas or slums, where most of the victims and enslaveables reside, also contributes. Additionally, lack of effective law enforcement may reflect the prevalence of loopholes in existing laws, allowing the perpetrators (and their collaborators) to exploit the law at the expense of their victims.[54] Fraudulent execution of existing laws in favor of the perpetrators and against MDS victims is likely to cause the victims to hide their "passive" and "forced" participation in illegal activities, such as prostitution and trafficking. Corrupt police officers and judges play a significant role in perpetuating MDS practices: collaborating with MDS perpetrators, accepting bribes or a share in the enslavement rent, and extorting, harassing, prosecuting the victims, and releasing them to MDS perpetrators, such as MDS traffickers and brothel owners (U.S. DOS, 2005a, Section 5).

The tendency of corrupt government officials, at the national and state levels, to shift government expenditures and other resources toward areas in which they can collect bribes more efficiently is likely to reduce government intervention against MDS practices (Lipset and Lenz, 2000). In addition, the

---

[54] In spite of national acts against MDS practices in India, such as the Immoral Trafficking Prevention Act (ITPA) of 1956 and the Bonded Labour System (Abolition) Act of 1976, such practices still exist. This is primarily due to the government's weak investigation and prosecution against MDS practices in India, in terms of insufficient numbers of convictions or sentences against MDS perpetrators and public officials who collaborate with MDS perpetrators. Much of this is due, in part, to endemic police corruption, and widespread corrupt local government in many states (U.S. DOS, 2006b, Section IV; Chakma, 2007, p. 36). In addition, reports show few sentences have been imposed under the Bonded Labour System (Abolition) Act of 1976. A significant trade-off occurs at the local level, between the prosecution of MDS perpetrators (e.g., businesses that employ bonded laborers) and the local government's need to collect taxes from these businesses – which, in turn, causes local government not to prosecute MDS perpetrators, or rescue MDS victims (U.S. DOS, 2005b, Section V).

prevalence of government corruption, especially low-level corruption (particularly at local levels in rural areas), provides a safer (or less risky) environment for illegal practices such as modern-day slavery, and reduces the risks and costs of such practices. This, in turn, increases the net enslavement rent (net of bribe or collaborating government officials' share in the enslavement rent) (Jeffrey, 2002). Such low-level/local corruption plays a crucial role in spreading and perpetuating MDS practices, in spite of national anti-MDS laws and policies (Coursen-Neff, 2003; Human Rights Watch, 1999). Additionally, in local and rural areas, the upper-class and influential groups (e.g., higher caste Hindus) can intimidate low-level government officials, such as police and judges, to serve their own interests, usually at the expense of the SC/ST. The lack of uniformity of formal rules, including personal laws between and within the same states (UNDP, 2004, p. 57), opens the door for strategic behaviors and schemes by MDS perpetrators, which usually take advantage of the poor and vulnerable. Recent reports show the Indian government's failure to demonstrate effective law enforcement, and to provide adequate local prosecution against MDS perpetrators who participate in the trafficking of MDS victims across state lines. It is difficult to investigate and prosecute these traffickers and perpetrators without the participation of, and support from, the national government and authorities (U.S. DOS, 2004a).

3.3.5 *Cultural factors:* Major cultural factors include the prevalence of informal norms, beliefs, and traditions (explained in Chapter 3) that marginalize certain group(s), making them more vulnerable to potential abuse, including enslavement.

Societies tend to follow certain embedded, and usually unquestionable, norms and traditions, even at the expense of violating formal laws and regulations, since traditions and customs tend to serve and sustain the interest of the elite or majority at the expense of the marginalized communities. This explains, in part, the continued discrimination against the SC/ST in India, ignoring the Constitution and subsequent anti-discrimination acts, since following the Hindu traditional norms serves the interests of the higher castes and precedes existing formal rules (Human Rights Watch, 2003; Thorat, 2002).

Strict social and cultural norms, such as the Hindu caste system in India, play a significant role in depriving marginalized communities such as the SC/ST from obtaining access to productive assets, education, and employment opportunities, especially in rural areas, where most of the SC/ST reside. Such deprivation of physical and social assets form vicious cycles of poverty that perpetuate the SC/ST's social and economic ostracism and vulnerability to discrimination, including MDS practices (Unni, 2001; Thorat, 2002). Examples of such cultural factors include the significant financial obligations associated with certain customs and traditions (e.g., dowry and funeral expenses) that are beyond the normal means of poor and vulnerable families. Embedded discrimination against certain groups, for example, the SC/ST, tends to provoke widespread abuse and violence against them. In certain communities, especially rural communities, women are still considered the property of men. Consequently, they are more prone to enslavement, and their children become vulnerable to modern-day slavery as well.[55] Such discriminating traditions explain in part the induced higher rate of female infanticide and the significantly higher rate of female child mortality, which, in turn, send a clear signal regarding the unwelcome status of females, and deepen and perpetuate women's and female children's vulnerability to modern-day slavery.

3.3.6 International factors: The international role in perpetuating MDS practices reflects, on one side, the international apathy toward such practices (as domestic or local problems), and the ineffective enforceability of many

---

[55] Examples of existing 'informal' discriminating traditions against women in India, especially in rural and marginalized areas, include the Sati (widow burning), *Devadasis* (the temple prostitutes), dowry (payments by females' parents to their in-laws, upon marriage), and aginipariksha (placing women's hands on fire to test their fidelity to their husbands) (U.S. DOS, 2002a).

international human rights and anti-discrimination conventions and laws. On the other side, it reflects the strong interest and effective demand by certain international participants such as international/foreign brothels, pornographers, pedophile rings, and slave traffickers, all of whom benefit from the availability of MDS practices, such as pedophilia, child pornography, and forced prostitution. The low cost of producing MDS products, and their exotic appeal (e.g., certain handmade consumer products, such as scarves, carpets, and glassware), boosts the effective demand for MDS products in international markets. This, in turn, attracts the interest and participation of some multinational corporations and international/foreign importers in MDS industries.

Certain misguided and controversial interventions, such as boycotting certain goods produced by child labor in LDCs, can lead to worse forms of MDS practices in LDCs, due to the lack of viable opportunities for these children or their families, such as free education and employment opportunities for their parents. Such international interventions may lead to the transformation of these children into enslaveables, forced into worse local, non-tradable MDS industries/sectors.

4. The Enslavement Rent and Social Costs of Modern-Day Slavery

The term 'enslavement rent' is used in this book to refer to the perpetrators' net gain from enslaving MDS victims. Measuring the enslavement rent is a complex and difficult task since modern-day slavery is illegal in most, if not all, countries and communities. Additionally, the wide spectrum of MDS practices, from low value-added activities such as hand-rolled beedi cigarettes or producing match boxes for local markets, to high value-added activities such as prostitution and pedophilia rings (which attract more affluent and foreign customers/tourists) causes enslavement rent to vary significantly across sectors and practices of modern-day slavery. The indispensable component of enslavement rent, which separate the enslavement rent from other forms or types of rents, is the forced participation of MDS victims in the MDS industries.[56] Significant social dead-weight welfare loss accompanies MDS because of the excess burden of MDS on MDS victims that results from their forced participation in MDS, which exceeds the MDS perpetrators' enslavement rent.

4.1 The perpetrators' share of enslavement rent

The crucial component of enslavement rent is the share of primary MDS perpetrators such as owners of brothels and sweatshops, adjusted for the costs and risks that accompany the enslavement process. The major source of the perpetrators' gains from MDS practices is the low production cost, especially in labor-intensive MDS industries, using cheap, if not free, labor. MDS perpetrators also gain from the regulation 'free' production environment, since most MDS practices are non-registered. This allows them to avoid registration and regulation requirements, taxes, and other related financial obligations or liabilities, especially in case of illegal MDS practices (prostitution, forced prostitution, child pornography, and pedophilia, in addition to other health-hazard industries, e.g., glassware, matches, and fireworks).

On the other hand, the perpetrators' major costs, and risks undertaken, include: the cost of recruiting or entrapping MDS victims, including payments to MDS traders/recruiters (usually a lump-sum payment); the cost of maintaining and training MDS victims; the cost of keeping/hiding the victims and denying the MDS practices; the cost of relocating MDS practices to avoid government inspectors, police, or NGO inspections; the collaborators' share of the enslavement rent; and, the risk of being caught and prosecuted. The indirect costs of MDS practices, such as bribery, sharing the enslavement rent with the

---

[56] Rent, generally, refers to the difference between the income generated from the use (or exploitation) of a factor of production (e.g., land, labor, capital) and the minimum cost required to use (or exploit) such a factor.

collaborators (e.g., politicians, judges, and police officers), and the costs of legal services, constitute most of the cost of MDS practices.

4.2 Distribution of enslavement rent

The list of potential recipients of enslavement rent varies from a single MDS perpetrator to a long list that includes active and passive, intended and unintended, and direct and indirect participants at different stages of production and consumption of MDS products or services. This list includes MDS recruiters (or traders), ultimate MDS perpetrators, and, to a lesser extent, security guards (or gangsters who protect the perpetrators' interest, intimidate MDS victims and their families, and prevent them from escaping or taking any actions against the perpetrators), public servants such as politicians, legislators, police officers, and judges who collaborate with MDS perpetrators, owners and users of other industries that use the slave-produced output as inputs, multinational or foreign corporations that use or import MDS products, and consumers of MDS products and services.

4.3 Social losses/costs of modern-day slavery

MDS practices bring about significant dead-weight loss in social welfare, due to the significant gap between MDS victims' losses and the enslavement rent extracted by the perpetrators.[57] The dead-weight loss represents the differences between the net present value of social welfare loss to the MDS victims and society overall, and the enslavement rent extracted by the MDS perpetrators. This gap is mostly due to MDS victims' forced participation, so that only part of the victims' costs and pain is transferred to the perpetrators, in the form of enslavement rent; the rest is non-transferable and non-recoverable dead-weight

---

[57] Deadweight loss represents the net loss to society associated with inefficiency in markets or transactions, for example, MDS practices in this case. The socially efficient level of MDS practices should be zero, i.e., absence of MDS practices. Accordingly, MDS practices generate higher costs/losses to society than enslavement rent extracted by MDS perpetrators.

loss to the society overall. The following list highlights the major losses to MDS victims and society overall:

- The physical pain and suffering inflicted on the victims in the process of enslavement;
- The mental health problems due to the victims' high stress and feelings of misery and hopelessness;
- The foregone value of opportunities such as education, and the stream of personal, social, and economic value added, that would have been produced if these victims were not enslaved.
- The victims' physical exposure to high-risk environments such as HIV/AIDS and other sexually-transmitted diseases in some MDS practices (e.g., forced prostitution, pedophilia, and pornography), and other health risks associated with hazardous environments (e.g., respiratory illness in firework, matchbox, carpet and scarf industries), and other work-related diseases and injuries, due to the victims young age, illness, and malnutrition;
- Stunted growth of MDS victims, some instances of which are accompanied by physical disabilities, especially for child victims of modern-day slavery. for examples, MDS victims of violent sexual acts and sexually-transmitted diseases, and/or physical damage in hazardous MDS practices, such as brick kilns, stone quarries, matches, fire work, and handmade carpets (U.S. DOS, 2007a, Section6c);
- The victims' sense of isolation, fear, and lack of trust in society and other people; and the victims' cycles of rejection by their families, and communities;
- The victims' deprivation of basic human rights to liberty, freedom, and, in extreme cases, life;

- Breakdown of social structures, in terms of separating the victims from their families, either physically or through MDS perpetrators' control over the victims;

- The perpetuation of MDS practices, lack of community and social support corrupt the enslaveables' perception and measurement of the rate of return on investment in their children's human capital (e.g., education and health). Such lack of human capital reduces the capabilities of the enslaveables, and thus deepens and perpetuates the vulnerability of the enslaveables and increases their vulnerability to MDS practices in the future (U.S. DOS, 2006b, Section I);

- MDS practices, especially those supported by collaborating agents from law enforcement, promote similar illegal practices such as organized crimes, at the expense of the enslaveables, the most vulnerable population groups (U.S. DOS, 2006b, Section I);

- MDS practices lead to erosion of government authority and beneficial institutions and the prevalence of corruption and bribery, which, in turn, restrain economic development and growth;

- Existing MDS practices tend to perpetuate the embedded unjust and oppressive norms and traditions, which, in turn, perpetuate the vulnerability of the enslaveables, and MDS practices.

Chapter 3

New Institutional Economic Analysis of

Modern-Day Slavery

If the institutional framework made the highest pay-offs for organizations' piracy, then organizational success and survival dictated that learning would take the form of being better pirates. Douglass North (1998, p. 21)

[. . .] we are still very ignorant about institutions. Oliver Williamson (2000, p. 595)

We must study the unique configurations of non-Western societies, their institutions. Economic anthropology is about the institutions surrounding the provision of the material necessities of existence to man. Frank Cancian (1966, p. 465)

The difficulty in defining a field for the so-called institutional economics is the uncertainty of meaning of an institution. Sometimes an institution seems to mean a framework of laws or natural rights within which individuals act like inmates. Sometimes it seems to mean the behavior of the inmates themselves. Sometimes anything additional to or critical of the classical or hedonic economics is deemed to be institutional. Sometimes anything that is "economic behavior" is institutional. Sometimes anything that is "dynamic" instead of "static," or a "process" instead of commodities, or activity instead of feelings, or mass action instead of individual action, or management instead of equilibrium, or control instead of laissez faire, seems to be institutional economics. John Commons (1931, p. 648)

Institutions play a crucial role in elucidating such a complex phenomenon as modern-day slavery. They are humanly devised constraints that structure human interactions. The three major categories of institutions are the informal institutions (or informal constraints), formal institutions (or formal rules or constraints), and the governance structure of transactions (or the play of the game). Informal institutions include the embedded norms, customs, mores, religions, and self–imposed codes-of-conduct in each society. Formal rules include statute laws, common laws, and regulations that determine the distribution of power across different levels of government in bureaucratic, executive, legislative, and judicial functions. The governance structure of the game refers to the play of the game, where contracts and their governance costs become the rules rather than the exceptions (North, 1994 and 1998; Williamson, 1993 and 2000).

Institutions allow societies and economies to deal with market failure and the pursuit of goals other than efficiency. The new institutional economics approach offers an explanation as to why the evolutions of individual countries – or certain groups within each country – differ from one other (Harris, et. al., 1998). According to North (1998, p. 17), "The new institutional economics is an attempt to incorporate a theory of institutions into economics." It does not replace the neo-classical theory; rather, it "...builds on, modifies, and extends neo-classical theory to permit it to come to grips with an entire range of issues that are beyond its ken." It opens up the terrain of genuinely inter-disciplinary analysis such as political science, religion, sociology, psychology, as well as economics. It ascribes an important role to ideologies and history, where present and future are connected to the past by the continuity of society's institutions (Dugger, 1995; Basu, 1986; Commons, 1931). It also encompasses the panoply of cultural characteristics used by anthropologists and sociologists to describe a society (Akerlof, 1976, p. 600).

Douglass North (1998, p. 20) underscores the role of bargaining in the distribution of institutional powers. He states, "Institutions are not necessarily or even usually created to be socially efficient; rather they, or at least the formal rules, are created to serve the interests of those with the bargaining power to create new rules." In essence, they are created for those who can extract "institutional" rent from the construction and perpetuation of these rules. Platteau (1994b, p. 787) shares a similar sentiment: "To the extent that rules and institutions are always a product of historical (social and political) processes working out their effect in a world characterized by imperfect and incomplete markets, there is no reason to expect these rules and institutions to be (even second-best) efficient." In an imperfect world, where information and contracts are far from ideal, transactions are not frictionless, and materials are scarce, "theft, predatory behavior, and violence displace mutual-gain production and exchanges (i.e., 'take' displaces 'make' and 'buy'). In such an economy, corrupt governments, subverted laws, special interests, and lawlessness and criminality are allowed to run rampant, taking the place of "a transparent, honest and strong government that impartially administers the laws and effectively maintains civic orders" (Kaufman, 2007, p. 14). Therefore, human interactions become instituted, socially constructed, and power[58] becomes a central construct in institutional economics (Granovetter, 1991, p. 76).

Akerlof (1976, p. 600) highlighted the role of indicators in making exchanges. "Some indicators owe their existence purely to social conventions rather than to economic information in almost all conventional economic models. In the case of caste, individuals' behavior toward others is predicted by their respective caste status." He continues to note that, "[t]he boundaries between sociology and economics are by no means clear: economic models can explain sociological phenomena, and sociological models can describe economic phenomena" (p. 611).

Platteau (1994a, p. 537) highlights the importance of social foundations: "The issue of social foundations or preconditions of the market has clearly a multidimensional character calling for a multidisciplinary perspective: no single discipline can honestly claim to have a decisive advantage in resolving it." Identifying the informal norms, Platteau finds that, "[t]he social fabric and the culture of human societies matter a great deal, and to the extent that norms and

---

[58] Power refers to the ability to satisfy one's preference. Personal political power, rather than the forces of impersonal supply and demand in the neoclassical economy, plays an important role in determining the distribution of rewards and costs of economic activities (Kaufman, 2007, p. 16).

cultural beliefs are rooted in historical processes, history necessarily determines the development trajectories of particular countries." (p. 535). In addition, he illustrates three rules (or equilibria): first, good (or honest) equilibrium; second; multiple equilibria, associated with the need to direct the society from a 'bad' equilibrium to a 'good' equilibrium; third, bad equilibrium, in which the society is entrapped in a unique bad/dishonest equilibrium. Institutions are involved, or used, in the second and third mechanisms (p. 535). MDS practices are examples of the third rule, where the victims are entrapped and forced to participate in activities that serve the interest of MDS perpetrators.

On the other hand, economic institutions can influence social interactions, and thus precipitate the evolution of institutional rules and norms by altering the returns to relationships, affecting the kind of sanctions, and changing the likelihood and outcomes of interactions of different types of people (Bowles, 1998). For example, the adverse effects of MDS practices may influence the preference sets of the enslaveables and MDS victims, making them more likely to be submissive and victimized, and less likely to oppose or reject such practices. Effective interventions that reduce the vulnerability of the enslaveables and MDS victims and empower them, and prosecute MDS perpetrators, should alter the evolution of rules and norms, in favor of the former enslaveables and MDS victims, instead.

The behavior of MDS victims and the enslaveables – behavior which may seem irrational – can be explained by psychologists, who view irrational behavior as predictable, and not totally random. Therefore, economic analysis should endeavor to incorporate observations of individuals who do not behave as economists assume they do, which is well stated by Akerlof and Dickens (1982, p. 307), "... we must translate psychological theory into concept amenable to incorporation into an economic model."

1. Classification and Levels of Institutions and Modern-Day Slavery

There are three main levels of institutions, in term of their structures, roles, and propensities to change. They are the informal institutions, formal institutions, and the governance of these institutions.

1.1 Informal institutions (or informal constraints)

It may appear that the tastes of persons of discriminating societies are so overwhelmingly biased in favor of discrimination that, relatively, the positive or negative effects of economic incentives are of only minor moment. George Akerlof (1976, p. 609)

Obedience to the norm will occur when the sanctions or discomfort are sufficiently great and sufficiently certain to make disobedience less immediately attractive than obedience. James Coleman (1987, pp. 141-42)

In stable pre-industrial economics, exchange may be influenced by culturally inherited economic roles... Social networks tend to fix the direction and magnitude of exchange flows. Marcel Fafchamps (2004, p. 20)

"... the institutional form of society affects its members and determines in large part the kind of persons they want to be as well as the kind of persons they are." John Rawls (1993, p. 269)

The informal institutions are prevailing social norms, cultural conventions, customs, traditions, religious doctrines, myths, taboos, and ethical principles, in addition to self-imposed codes of conducts (North, 1998; Kaufman, 2007). These institutions are usually taken as given. They develop through evolutionary processes of gradual feedbacks and adjustments, and tend to change very slowly over time, in centuries and millennia (Williamson, 2000; Kasper and Streit, 1998). Informal institutions reveal the gradual acceptance, the power structure, and the weighted conviction in such norms over time, regardless of how ethical or fair.

The languages and mental models formed the informal constraints that defined the institutional framework of the tribe and were passed down intergenerationally as the customs, taboos, myths that provide the

60

continuity of culture and forms part of the key to path dependence. Douglass North (1998, p. 20).[59]

Prevailing informal institutions influence individuals' mental models with regard to their shared perceptions, expectations, and interpretation of the world around them (Denzau and North, 1993). Informal institutions that victimize a certain population group (or class) not only distort their mental models, but also, offer other group(s) the opportunity to gain at the expense of these victims. The winners enjoy an additional mental edge that can be utilized to extract 'distributional' rent when transacting or contracting with the victims of such institutions. Institutional path dependence underscores the enduring influence of continued cultural, social, and economic systems and practices over time, which, in turn, highlights how history influences current conditions. "In everyday language the individuals and organizations with bargaining power as a result of the institutional framework have a crucial stake in perpetuating the system" (North, 2002, p. 3). People continue to act based on how things were done in the past.

Informal institutions explain the presence of embedded norms and traditions that perpetuate phenomena such as modern-day slavery. North (1994, p. 363) remarks: "History demonstrates that ideas, ideologies, myths, dogmas, and prejudices matter; and an understanding of the way they evolve is necessary for further progress in developing a framework to understand societal changes." Marcel Fafchamps demonstrates how patterns of exchange become internalized as culturally hereditary economic roles, which, in turn, sustain the vulnerability of the enslaveable groups (2004, p. 20). Platteau differentiates between limited-groups morality and generalized morality and their role in social phenomena such as MDS. Limited group morality reflects morals that are restricted to individuals with whom one has a close identification. In contrast, generalized morality is

---

[59] "Mental models refer to the internal representations that individual cognitive systems create to interpret the environment; institutions are the external (to the mind) mechanisms individuals create to structure and order the environment" (North, 1994, p. 363).

morals applicable to outsiders, not necessarily allied through personal family, caste, or ethnic links (1994b, p. 770).

Cultural differences play a crucial role in explaining the state of marginalized groups (enslaveables) in different societies, at different historic times, and in different geographic regions. They help explain the different relationships between people and their surrounding physical and social environments. Exploring individualist and collectivist cultures explains in detail people's behaviors within and across societies/communities (Triandis 2001 and 1995).

In collectivist cultures, people think of themselves as interdependent within their groups (such as family, tribe, religion, or country). "They are more likely to give priority to the goals of their in-group than to their personal goals" (Triandis and Trafimow 2001, p. 261). They think and communicate as groups, rather than individuals, and they are more likely to give priority to the goals of the group, and their culture's language does not require the use of "I" and "You". In contrast, people in individualist cultures thinks of themselves as independent of the in-groups; they give priority to their personal goals and are likely to use "I" and "You" (p. 261). Platteau (1994b, p. 789) verifies this notion: "Collectivist cultures have shown less dynamism because they have not been subject to as much pressure for change ... as the individualistic cultures of the West."

Generally, people in individualist cultures are taught to be independent, creative, and self-expressive. They are encouraged to make decisions on their own, with less or no attention to the views of others, and are more likely to confront in-group members with whom they disagree. In contrast, people in collectivist cultures are taught to be obedient, nurturing, interdependent, and cooperative. They are likely to put the collective goals of the in-group ahead of their own personal goals (Triandis and Trafimow 2001, p. 261). They are also taught to conform to in-group norms, and to subordinate their need to the collective needs. They are also more sensitive to rejection, and have less need to be unique (Dayan, Doyle, and Markiewicz, 2001, pp. 767-68). The individualist-collectivist balance leans toward the individualist cultures in the US and Western Europe, and toward the collectivist cultures in South/South East Asia, the Middle East, Sub-Saharan Africa, and Central/ South America. At the personal level, there are individualists and collectivists in all cultures; however, more people lean toward being individualists in individualist cultures, and toward being collectivists in collectivist cultures. In summary, people in dominantly individualist cultures, supported by formal rules and informal institutions, are more likely to confront people with whom they disagree and to emphasize their goals and needs above others in the groups. In collectivist cultures, however, they are more likely to conform to and obey the in-group norms and boundaries and to subordinate their need to those of others (p. 768). This explains the ongoing presence of certain phenomena, such as MDS, in many collectivist LDCs and in collectivist communities in LDCs, regardless of how appalling these phenomena are.

Low-caste groups are more likely to be marginalized and harmed in collectivist societies that are caste-based, such that the distributional effect of existing cultural norms and cultural boundaries favor the upper castes at the expense of the lower castes and SC/ST members in these societies. Low-caste and SC/ST-members' responses will reflect their individualist-collectivist position. Generally, SC/ST and low-caste members are likely to conform to the cultural norms, regardless of how discriminating or degrading, in collectivist cultures, since they are taught to do so, and because of the severity of the collective punishments of not conforming to these cultural norms, boundaries, and practices.

The Hindu social caste system in India provides a typical example of informal institutions that assert the social and economic rights and the superiority of the higher Hindu castes at the expense of the SC/ST, who remain "outcaste, ostracised, ghettoised, and socially boycotted" (Guru, 2004, p. 757). For example,

Dharma, meaning 'to sustain' or 'fixed position,' is "the most central, the most persisting, and the most highly valued concept in Indian traditional polity" (Bondurant, 1966, p. 5). It implies the duties and rights of different caste members in society (ibid). Furthermore, economic reward may favor those who follow such prevailing social customs; and give economic reasons why such societal norms may endure (Akerlof, 1976, p.617).

In addition, the devalued status of women demonstrates another dimension of informal traditions (or constraints). Practices such as the *devadasis* (temple prostitutes or dancers),[60] *dowry* (payment by the bride's parents to the groom's family, upon marriage), *and sati* (the burning of widows on the funeral pyres of their husbands), also occur, especially in rural regions. Such informal traditions explain, in part, why 56 percent of surveyed women said that domestic violence is justified, and why the majority of rapes were never reported to authorities.[61] Such an informal environment tends to distort the structure of the victims' mental models, so they become more likely to accept such informal constraints and act accordingly.

George Akerlof (1976), in his analysis of the economics of castes in India, underlines the importance of recognizing the historical perspective, which attempts to explain the stability (or disappearance) of institutions over a long period of time. Denzau and North (1993) emphasize the role of cultural heritage as a means of reducing the divergence in the mental models among the same groups. Such cultural heritages, "constitute a means for the intergenerational transfer of unifying perceptions" (p. 8). According to Denzau and North, ideas

---

[60] *Devadasis* literally means "female servant of God," usually belongs to the Dalit community, and still exists in southern stated in India. These girls cannot marry and they are forced to have sex with temple priests. They become prostitutes for the upper caste community members, and eventually, they are sold to urban brothels. There are about 5,000 to 15,000 girls auctioned and sold secretly every year (Human Rights Watch, 1999, pp. 150-52).

[61] For more details, see De Bary (1998) and U.S. DOS (2000a).

matter since such ideologies "provide more closely shared perceptions and ordering of the environment" (p. 11). "Ideas matter and the way by which ideas evolve and are communicated is the key to developing useful theory which will expand our understanding of the performance of societies both at a moment of time and over time. At a moment of time, the argument implies that institutions and the belief structure are critical constraints on those making choices and are, therefore, an essential ingredient of model building" (p. 15). On one hand, these embedded informal institutions explain the limited success of short or medium term interventions, since the informal roots of modern-day slavery may outlast these short-lived interventions. On the other hand, they emphasize the importance of long-term intervention and commitments to initiate or continue the process of transforming or reversing these unfair and unethical informal institutions.

Governments are less likely to initiate policies to intervene with informal institutions, since the success, or even the progress, of such interventions in transforming or altering long-term informal institutions is difficult to materialize or even measure, given the short-term structure and duration of governments.

While informal institutions are considered constant (or given) in the short- and medium- terms, economic institutions may influence the structure of social interactions – and thus the evolution of norms – by altering the return to relationships, affecting the kinds of sanctions, and changing the likelihood of interactions for different types of people (Bowles, 1998). The adverse effect of modern-day slavery on the enslaved and the enslaveables may influence their preference, and make them lower their expectations and outlooks, especially if there is a long history of slavery and discrimination in their country. Conversely, the gradual influence of proper and fair economic institutions on the evolution of informal norms, stresses the need for immediate interventions by government, domestic and international non-government, and civil-society organizations. Such interventions can lead to the transformation or reversal of the existing inefficient and unfair informal institutions, however slowly and gradually.

1.2 Formal institutions (or formal rules or formal constraints)

The formal institutions refer to the polity, judiciary, laws, and regulations, etc. They are designed and formally enforced to reflect the distribution of power across different levels of government in bureaucratic, executive, legislative, and judicial functions, and usually mirror the power structure in society (Jeffrey, 2002; Kasper and Streit, 1998; North, 1990, 1994 and 1998; Williamson, 2000). Studies and official evidence from India show that the behavior of higher caste Hindus is governed by the prevailing informal institutions of the Hindu caste system, rather than by India's formal institutions, such as the Constitution and other subsequent laws (Thorat, 2002). Changing the formal rules is typically a medium- to long-term process.[62]

The self-interested, rent-seeking, MDS perpetrators, with superior information and social capital, usually take advantage of such distorted and incomplete formal rules to maximize their share of contract or transaction rent at the expense of their victims who are illiterate, poor, and desperate (Harris, et. al., 1998, p. 6). In such cases, the outcomes of these contracts or transactions are likely to be socially inefficient; however, they generate distributional effect that rewards the perpetrators.[63] On the contrary, MDS victims are not only deprived of any rent, but also are worse off due to their suffering from physical, mental, and emotional abuse, all non-recoverable. The latter part of the perpetrators' rent is unique to modern-day slavery, due to the forced participation of MDS victims.

1.3 Governance structure of transactions

---

[62] It took England about 140 years (from 1830 to 1970) to prohibit child labor and raise the minimum working age to 16. Historical experience in the U.S. and Europe show that a mix of economic, technological, social and legal factors acted together to eliminate child labor (Hasnat, 1995).

[63] According to Swinnerton and Rogers (1999), the distribution axiom of child labor, and enslavement, emphasizes the vulnerability of the enslaveables due to the skewed distribution of income and wealth in society.

The governance structure of transactions refers to the play of the game, where contracts, and the costs of governing them, become the rules rather than the exceptions. These costs lead to very remarkable, but rather complex, sets of outcomes of such contracts, due to the built–in contractual hazards and the lack of sufficient safeguards. Adverse selection is an example of a contractual (or transactional) hazard, in which the MDS perpetrators are the first to offer loans, cash advances, and employment and marriage promises/offers, to exploit the enslaveables later in MDS practices. Moral hazard is another example, where the enslaveables and MDS victims (the "principals") do not observe the actions of MDS perpetrators (the "agents") that take place after initiating the transaction (e.g., after delivering the cash advance or loan, or transporting MDS victims to the distant employment or marriage).

It may take a year to a decade to re-examine and re-arrange the governing structure of transactions (Williamson, 2000). Examples of the play of the game include incomplete and asymmetric information, the presence or absence of viable alternatives (or opportunities) to the parties involved, the waiting game, and the repeated game effect (covered later in this chapter).

Information plays a crucial role in the governance structure of the game, since it is costly, incomplete, and distributed asymmetrically among the parties of contracts/transactions. In the case of modern-day slavery, the perpetrators have a superior position (an information "edge") that they utilize to extract information rent at the expense of those with inferior position, namely, the enslaveables and MDS victims. Incomplete contracts/transactions serve the perpetrators' interest because of the perpetrators' well-designed sets of ex-post responses to MDS victims' reactions and possible government/NGO interventions. Furthermore, the perpetrators can enforce the terms that suit their interests and disregard the ones protecting MDS victims – victims who cannot afford to have the terms enforced or are uninformed about their interests or rights from the start. The perpetrators can also impose and enforce non-contractual terms, as long as they increase their payoff. Oliver Williamson (2000) summarizes the situation thusly: "contract as mere promise, unsupported by credible commitments, will not be self-enforcing" (p. 601).

Interaction among the above three levels of institutions is dominated by the influence of the longer set of institutions, so that the informal rules influence the structure of formal rules, which, in turn, influence the governance of the game. The reverse feedback effect is relatively weak and at best slow, unless radical changes take place in society that may bring different sets of formal rules and a different perspective toward changing the existing informal rules. Without due intervention, the successful deviant behaviors of MDS perpetrators may develop new trends. Gradually, such trends become ex-deviants and the perpetrators become ex-deviants, and eventually may be considered successful individuals and leaders (Bowles, 1998).

2. New Institutional Economic Analysis of Modern-Day Slavery

The new institutional economics approach plays a crucial role in explaining the prevalence of phenomena such as modern-day slavery in certain countries or societies, especially in LDCs. This approach should be utilized in the process of designing and implementing interventions that respond effectively to the roots, dynamics, symptoms, and outcomes of MDS practices.

The embedded informal norms, formal rules, and the prevalence of asymmetric information and incomplete contracts in MDS practices in LDCs highlight the importance of applying the new institutional economic analysis to modern-day slavery. The following analysis highlights the main effects that pertain to MDS practices in LDCs, with reference to the primary participants and institutional levels associated with each effect.

2.1 Information asymmetry/gap and information rent

Information rent refers to the advantage accrued to the party having an informational advantage over the other party, at their expense (Sykuta and Cook, 2001, p. 1274). One may think of information as the output of a production process (or function) where the inputs are the accumulated information and current effort is exerted to acquire more information and improve the quality of such information. The output is the accumulation of processed information and its efficiency, which, in turn, leads to a higher value of information rent. With respect to modern-day slavery, information rent is a function of the information gap between the perpetrators and MDS victims; the larger the information gap, the larger the information rent and, consequently, the larger the perpetrators' enslavement rent, gained at the expense of the enslaveables and MDS victims. Not only does this explain the strong incentive for perpetrators to exert more effort to accumulate more information to widen the information gap (given the level of information held by the MDS victims), but it also explains the perpetrator's incentive to hold the enslaved and enslaveables' information base to a minimum level, or to seek out (or choose among) the least informed victims. Also, it is reasonable to assume that the perpetrators provide the enslaveables with false information to widen the information gap. Platteau (1994a, pp. 541-543) highlights the role of information gaps and time lags in cheating behaviors. A considerable amount of information is required if co-operative games (or transactions) are to be played (executed). This may explain why the enslaveables are significantly less informed about the characteristics of MDS schemes with MDS perpetrators. Time lags in transactions between MDS perpetrators and the enslaveables also give the perpetrators a crucial tool to entrap their MDS victims and force them to participate in MDS practices. MDS perpetrators can afford the information cost (in contrast to the enslaveables), and take advantage of transaction time lags to entrap their victims and perpetuate MDS practices.

The theory of asymmetric information and incomplete contracting leads to asymmetries between those on the short side of market, such as MDS perpetrators and their collaborators (who are able to secure all the transactions they desire), and those on the long side of the market, such as the enslaveables and MDS victims (who may be unable to secure any transactions at all) (Bowles, 1998). This asymmetry increases the MDS perpetrator's information rent, and, consequently, the enslavement rent.

> [w]hen the asymmetrical character of information distribution is taken into account, it is no longer legitimate to view agents as socially unrelated automatons reacting parametrically to the signals of the market. Jean-Philippe Platteau (1994a, p. 554)

The perpetrators seek to gather specific information about the enslaveables, such as the enslaveables' level of desperation, the types of crises that actually or potentially affect them, the potential impact of such crises on them, and their information base. Natural crises such as floods, typhoons, and droughts may cause significant losses to homes, crops, livestock, and human lives. Personal crises such as the loss of a parent, severe sickness, or excessive cultural duties like dowry payments (for brides in India) present different types of information to the perpetrators; information regarding the severity, frequency, and duration of such crises is valuable input to the perpetrators. The perpetrators also invest in gathering information about the legal structure, such as property rights laws, the level and spread of government corruption, the justice system, the structure of law enforcement, and the levels of law enforcement. The amount of information obtained from previous actions and responses of government officials, judges, police officers, and other public servants to previous MDS practices, and the responses to current MDS practices by other perpetrators are of significant informational value. The perpetrators' gathering of such information continues as long as the expected net marginal information rent is positive or above a preset level.

Meanwhile, investing in information is a luxury the MDS victims cannot afford, due to their initial position (illiterate and poor), and their desperation (urgent need for help after a crisis, accompanied by a lack of viable alternatives). They are more likely to direct their efforts toward immediate sources of help, rather than toward gathering information. Additionally, they feel that society and prevailing informal and formal institutions have failed and abandoned them, if not victimized them, as well. The above factors restrict the enslaveables' ability and willingness to invest in information, and, consequently, limit their competency, widening the information gap between them and the perpetrators, which, in turn, increases the enslavement rent.

2.2 The desperation effect

The desperation effect refers to the hopelessness of the enslaveables, which makes them more vulnerable to potential abuse and enslavement. Contributing to this effect is the lack of – or insufficient relief from – the government or surrounding community, and the lack of other viable second sources such as lending or employment options (discussed later in this chapter), especially when adverse shocks cause complete or significant loss of income and assets. Other factors that contribute to deepening the enslaveables' desperation include the presence of adverse informal institutions that perpetuate the dehumanization and abuse of victims (based on race, gender, social caste, ethnicity, etc.), the spread of illiteracy and the resulting informational gap, and previous disappointments and letdowns. The environment created by these factors, in addition to the discriminating/marginalizing embedded cultural and the social constraints, is likely to diminish the enslaveables' cognitive resources, in terms of the time and attention required to evaluate their choices (Denzau and North, 1993). The perpetrators exploit the enslaveables' weariness, lack of viable resources, desperation, and diminished cognitive resources in order to extract more enslavement rent. Depending on their level of desperation, the enslaveables are likely to accept any offer or promise of loans or employment from MDS perpetrators without being able to negotiate or understand the transaction's information/terms or the complexity associated with such transactions (Williamson, 1993 and 2000).

In the case of desperation and lack of viable options, the enslaveables will engage in transactions if, given their bounded rationality, the immediate relief or gain (or just the promise of relief or gain) exceeds their 'distorted' perception of the future costs associated with such MDS transactions. Bounded rationality refers to individuals who normally make use of a subset of the decision's attributes as part of their decisions, rather than full rationality, when they take all attributes of the decision into consideration (Korobkin, 2003, p. 1203). The desperation effect makes the enslaveables more vulnerable to hurried decisions because of their dire state and urgent need for relief, in addition to the lack of other viable options. They are likely to accept any offers of immediate relief (such as cash advance or loan) or a promise of relief from MDS perpetrators, which may harm their interests and well-being later on.

In summary, extreme poverty, lower social status, limited access to the justice system, and the widespread corruption of police and other public servants, especially in rural regions, are all likely to trap the enslaveables in desperate circumstances. This desperation makes them accept immediate offers from MDS perpetrators, and deters them from reporting MDS practices to the police, for fear of retribution from corrupt police officers and/or their collaboration with MDS perpetrators.[64]

2.3 Forced participation

Forced participation of MDS victims is the fundamental characteristic of modern-day slavery, in which the perpetrators impose their will on the victims. It takes place once the tricked enslaveables become exposed and bound to the

---

[64] The Asian Centre for Human Rights reports many examples of police failing to protect the Dalits from atrocities by the upper castes, in addition to direct police participation in atrocities against the Dalits (Chakma, 2007).

perpetrators' set of rules and penalty/punishment schemes. Resistance or lack of participation by MDS victims is deterred by the credible threat of severe punishments such as beating, burning, detention, rape, and, in extreme cases, killing, especially when supported by credible threat records. The punishment scheme is utilized to force the victims' continuing participation, and, therefore, to sustain the stream of enslavement rent. Furthermore, MDS perpetrators usually extend their threats and punishments to the victims' relatives to ensure the victims continued submission, which, in turn, ensures the continuation of the enslavement rent. Examples of MDS practices that require forced participation include excessive quotas, long working hours, hazardous and unsafe working environments, and participation in illegal activities such as forced prostitution and pedophilia.

Coercion refers to the choice between different alternatives that reduce the utility, yet one of them is too costly to choose, for example, a death threat, or severe physical harm to self or loved ones. Sociologists distinguish between the actual exercise of physical force and the threat of such force. Both engage the victim in involuntary acts (Basu, 1986, pp. 274-75).

By increasing revenues and decreasing costs, the perpetrators exploit the victims' coerced participation, in order to extract more enslavement rent. They can increase their revenues by imposing excessive quotas to be produced, supplied, or served by the victims, according the different types of MDS practices. They, also, can lower their costs by forcing the victims to work at, or near, minimum direct and indirect costs. 'Unreasonable commands' and 'unwilling obedience' that refer to the acts of MDS perpetrators and MDS victims, respectively, are what separate MDS practices from normal exchanges or transactions that are associated with 'reasonable commands,' and 'willing obedience.' The involuntary choice responds to the individual imposition by MDS perpetrators, and/or the collective imposition by collective actions (Commons, 1931, p. 653). Furthermore, MDS perpetrators (and their collaborators, e.g., corrupt police officers) can also threaten or punish the relatives of the MDS victims as a pressure tool to ensure MDS victims' obedience and participation in MDS industries (Human Rights Watch, 1999).

The victims fear they will be devastated if they refuse to cooperate with the MDS perpetrators. With the absence of other viable options, the victims may accept a bad offer, if the other options yield worse outcomes, such as starvation or destitution. Any offer that matches the enslaveables reservation/threshold level is likely to be accepted by the enslaveables (Basu, 1986, p. 268). Desperate enslaveables, shortsighted by the immediate gain (e.g., cash advance), are typically unaware of the entrapment present in the schemes of MDS perpetrators. The enslaveables and MDS victims know that if they violate the commitment to abide by these imposed constraints, regardless of how unfair, they will pay an excessive price for their actions. They know that if they rebel, they will be punished very harshly, so they do not dare disobey in the first place.

Generally, the violation of collective rules and norms, especially by vulnerable groups such as the enslaveables, in collectivist societies, exposes the vulnerable violators to harsh informal and formal punishments, since such violations confront or oppose the main tenets in these societies. Such harsh punishments serve as a signal to other enslaveables or MDS victims not to rebel against, or confront MDS perpetrators.

MDS perpetrators (and upper caste members) know that MDS victims and the enslaveables are aware of what MDS perpetrators (and upper caste members) can do when MDS victims (and SC/ST) rebel or disobey. In addition to direct, or threats of, physical punishment, exclusion from collective activities, social boycott and social shame represent other forms of collective punishments inflicted when the enslaveables and MDS victims fail to participate (or, more precisely, obey orders) accordingly (Guinnane, 2005, pp. 9-10).

2.4 The waiting game

MDS perpetrators, prepared for the contingencies associated with MDS practices, are likely to invest in gathering specific information about interventions (by government and non-government agencies, such as human rights and civil-society organizations) in terms of their structures, intensity, time and length of inspection. More importantly, the perpetrators also investigate any constraints that may impede the effectiveness of such interventions. Information, time, funding, and personal interests are all examples of constraints that usually hinder the effectiveness of these interventions. For example, the longer the time spent on MDS cases, the less time and other resources are available that can be directed toward related projects of interest to the intervening organizations and their representatives. Furthermore, due to the harsh MDS environment usually present in poor and unsafe locations, only a few agencies and personnel may have genuine interest in such unpleasant practices and the high degrees of risk associated with their intervention. In such a process, the person who is more driven and willing to last longer usually prevails. Consequently, interventions are more likely to be ineffective because of the constraints explained above, the high degree of readiness on the part of MDS perpetrators, and the fact that MDS perpetrators thrive and extract more enslavement rent in such unpleasant and unsafe environments.[65]

This effect also highlights the importance of independent organizations such as civil society and human rights organizations that have continuing local presence, and are well-driven to serve the interest of the enslaved and enslaveables and to counteract the perpetrators' tactics of outlasting and diminishing the effectiveness of other interventions.

2.5 Pressure (or interest) groups

---

[65] MDS perpetrators/employers usually stop using children and bonded laborers, or make them stop working prior to, and during, inspections. The perpetrators/employers usually know about such inspections ahead of time (Human Rights Watch, 2003).

The organized pressure group arises because differential advantage is expected to be secured through the political process, and, in turn, differential advantages for particular groups are produced because of the existence of organized activity. James Buchanan and Gordon Tullock (1967, p. 287)

This effect reflects the role of pressure groups in influencing and lobbying public policy for the purpose of sustaining or deterring MDS practices. Generally, MDS perpetrators can form interest groups, through pecuniary and non-pecuniary bribes or shares in the enslavement rent, with other existing interest groups and government officials at different government levels. The purpose of these interest groups is to influence corruptible government officials (judges, police, and other bureaucrats who have access to information regarding MDS practices) to act according to the interests of MDS perpetrators. These corrupt officials have a crucial stake in perpetuating MDS practices (North, 1998, pp. 19-20). Effective interest groups lower the risk and, consequently, the cost of engaging in MDS practices, which, in turn, increase the enslavement rent that is now distributed among a larger circle of MDS perpetrators, including the pressure groups and corrupt government officials. Furthermore, the special interest effect argues that the political process will favor issues that concentrate benefits upon small groups of people (MDS perpetrators and their collaborators) but also spread costs across many other voters or larger sectors of the population, such as the enslaveables.

On the other hand, the interest-group effect underscores the presence of other agencies, such as human rights, civil society, and government and non-government organizations (NGOs) that aim to serve and lobby on behalf of MDS victims and the enslaveables, prosecute MDS perpetrators, eradicate MDS practices, and initiate/promote the development of marginalized regions. Their presence is extremely crucial for counterbalancing the domestic pressure groups (MDS perpetrators and their collaborators) that benefit from the discriminating informal norms and formal rules. Interest groups with a pro-victim agenda, such as NGOs and civil-society organizations, play a significant role in augmenting the enslaveables' social capital, in terms of supporting honest behavior, exposing immoral and illegal acts of both private and public agents, and continuing to press for the effective enforcement of laws. All of these efforts serve to increase the costs of MDS practices, and build effective social networks that support and protect the interest of the enslaveables.

Interest groups usually intervene through gathering and disseminating information, mobilizing public awareness, and providing legal support and protection for the victims and enslaveables, while also reporting MDS practices and perpetrators to the authorities. They can also act as pressure groups to lobby for, and secure the passage of, legislation that supports the cause of the enslaveables and MDS victims, on one hand, and prosecutes MDS perpetrators and their collaborators, on the other (Buchanan and Tullock, 1967, pp. 285-86). Effective interventions of interest groups on behalf of the enslaveables and MDS victims should reduce the enslaveables' vulnerability. It should also increase the costs of MDS practices for MDS perpetrators and their collaborators, thereby shrinking the enslavement rent and discouraging MDS practices.

2.6 The repeated-game effect

This effect illustrates the MDS perpetrators' efficiency and knowledge gained from repeating the processes of enslavement with new MDS victims, enslaveables, and government and non-government interventions. It also explains the seemingly unpredictable and irrational behaviors of the enslaveables and MDS victims. MDS victims learn from the repeated outcomes of previous experiences, which, in turn, influence their mental models and their expected responses to future transactions (Bloch and Rao, 2000). Repeated letdowns, failure to receive justice, and credible threats, supported by severe punishments by the perpetrators (in response to victims' previous complaints, resistance, or escape) are more likely to heighten the enslaveables' vulnerability and reduce MDS victims' resistance and rejection of MDS practices. In such cases, MDS victims are less likely to resist or report such practices.[66] Moreover, the information regarding the lack of, or ineffective, interventions against MDS practices reduces the costs and risks associated with these practices, which, in turn, increases the perpetrators' enslavement rent and encourages new similar practices. Furthermore, the perpetrators' repeated process of entrapping the enslaveables and transforming them into MDS victims improves the perpetrators' efficiency, lowering the costs and risks of such practices.

Alternatively, repeated and effective interventions against MDS practices increase the costs and risk of such practices, which, in turn, cut the enslavement rent through deterring MDS practices, punishing the perpetrators, freeing the victims, and empowering (or reducing the vulnerability of) the enslaveables.

Repetition mechanisms present in normal transactions – those that ensure the repetition and continuity of transactions between the transaction's agents and facilitate new or future transactions – do not exist and are not needed in MDS transactions, due to the non-repetitive transactions between MDS perpetrators and the same MDS victims. Harsh punishments, supported by creditable threats, serve as a daily deterrent against any rebellion or laziness on the part of MDS victims. MDS perpetrators compel MDS victims' responses by coercion, since MDS victims are entrapped and lack viable alternatives.

Typically, MDS perpetrators avoid repeated tactics with the same victims. This explains, in part, why MDS perpetrators target victims from disconnected and marginalized groups/communities. The victims' shame may prevent them from sharing their fates with other potential victims. In extreme cases, MDS perpetrators may not need to hide their bad reputation (in terms of changing their schemes). Their knowledge of the enslaveables' dire need for what the MDS

---

[66] Human Rights Watch (1999) reported examples of local police corruption and abuse of India's Dalits, such as the police's refusal to register the Dalits' complaints against upper-castes or to enforce legislation the protect Dalits, in addition to acting as agents for powerful upper-caste groups (p. 23). Other cases of corruption are cited in U.S. DOS (2007a, Section 5).

perpetrators can offer (e.g., cash for loans, advance payment for employment contracts, or marriage) and the lack of viable alternatives for the enslaveables, gives the MDS perpetrators the upper hand. MDS perpetrators can punish their victims if they violate the perpetrators' rules. Any non-cooperative act by the enslaveables or MDS victims is typically met with severe punishment – as the enforcement mechanism – by the MDS perpetrators.

2.7 Government corruption and public-choice theory

Public choice theory refers to the behavior of government officials, and public servants' acts, which satisfy their own self-interests instead of the public's interests. This effect refers to the corruption of government officials (politicians, judges, and other public servants) stemming from their rent-seeking aspirations. It is based on the rational choice model, which explains non-market decision-making by applying economic theory to political science (Hill, 1999, p. 1; Krueger, 1974, p. 292). According to this model, government officials, instead of seeking and implementing policies and procedures to protect the interest of the enslaveables and MDS victims, exploit their positions, authority, and information regarding MDS practices to collaborate with MDS perpetrators for the purpose of earning and sustaining a share in the enslavement rent; another form of rent-seeking behavior.[67]

Low pay, lack of transparency, widespread corruption, and lack of effective punishments are among the main factors that advance the public choice effect in LDCs. Officials' low pay tends to increase the marginal value of the bribe or share in the enslavement rent, while the other factors reduce the risk and cost of participating in MDS practices. These officials are likely to be more informed about these practices (than non-corrupt officials are), since they can exploit such an information gap to sustain or increase their shares of enslavement

---

[67] For further analysis of the theory of public choice, see Buchanan (2003), Grindle and Thomas (1991), Jeffrey (2002), Khan (1996), McChesney (1987 and 1997), and Noll (1988).

rent, increasing their payoff, and reducing the risks of their collaboration with MDS perpetrators.

In addition to the self-initiated self-interest and rent–seeking behaviors of government officials, influential landlords and upper-caste politicians (and MDS perpetrators and their collaborators) are successful in manipulating and intimidating these officials, especially low-level officials, to act in their favor. People of influence (e.g., influential upper castes, MDS perpetrators), if they so wish, can induce or pressure other people (e.g., public servants, police and judges) to do them favors, regardless of how unfair these favors are (Basu, 1986). Accordingly, the self-interest government officials become the victims of rent-seeking behaviors by the more influential dominant classes. Ultimately, such practices take place at the expense of vulnerable and marginalized groups, especially in rural regions (Jeffrey, 2002; Khan, 1996; Human Rights Watch, 1999 and 2005).

It is important to differentiate between "grand corruption," involving massive sums of monetary transactions that usually attract significant public attention and intervention, and "retail corruption," which is associated with small monetary transactions in low-level local districts and rural areas, tied to low–level officials. Most of the high-level officials' practices are high-margin, raising large sums from few people, such as key MDS perpetrators who extract exorbitant enslavement rents, whereas, the low-level officials' practices are volume-based, more frequently collected from large numbers of people, including volume MDS perpetrators, who extract low-margin enslavement rent. Retail corruption is less likely to attract attention, and, consequently, it is likely to continue. This process perpetuates local MDS practices and schemes at the expense of the very poor and marginalizes residents in poor local and rural areas (Gopakumar, 1998; Gupta, 1995). The very poor, who cannot afford to bribe the low-level local officials, are usually left behind. Meanwhile, the ability of MDS perpetrators to bribe local officials makes modern-day slavery a routine practice.[68] Gupta (1995) underscores the importance of retail corruption, "for the majority of Indian citizens, the most immediate context for encountering the state is provided by their relationship with government bureaucracies at the local level" (p. 378), especially since high-ranking officials do not usually reside in poor areas. Gupta also highlights the role of cultural capital,[69] often mastered by corrupt and influential people, such as MDS perpetrators, since it requires a great deal of performance competence and experience. The enslaveables typically lack such cultural capital, required to negotiate with corrupt local officials (p. 381).

Studies show that when central resources are delegated to local organizations, the elite tend to appropriate whatever they need, and leave the leftovers to the poor. The advantages of community-based programs can be outweighed by accountability problems, especially when communities have information deficiencies, or there is no functioning democracy at the local level – mostly due to corrupt local leaders (Abraham and Platteau, 2001, pp. 2-3).

Similar to the repeated-game effect, the public-choice effect explains the MDS victims and enslaveables' hesitance/reluctance to seek government intervention, because of their fear that such an act may inflict further harm on them.

MDS victims will not involve legal institutions in the resolution of crimes against them if they anticipate that the benefits from such legal actions will fall short of the costs of seeking such actions. MDS victims and the enslaveables will not seek legal recourse when the costs of legal action are high. Such costs include lawyer's fees, high bribes to agents of authority, significant fear of reprisal from MDS perpetrators, lack of access to the legal system, and their personal shame: a

---

[68] Human rights experts report discrimination and custodial torture of the poor who cannot afford legal assistance (U.S. DOS, 2005a, Section 1d).

[69] Cultural capital refers to certain advantages, such as knowledge and attitudes, which give certain people a higher status in communities, and make them more likely to succeed

typical case of cognitive dissonance (Fafchamps, 2004, p. 29). These factors discourage the enslaveables and MDS victims from seeking legal redress. In addition, corrupt officials and government agencies play a vital role in sustaining MDS practices, by minimizing the enslaveables' use of (and trust in) the legal system to obtain government intervention against MDS perpetrators and practices.

2.8 Access to viable alternatives (or second sources)

The effective presence and accessibility of second sources such as lending facilities, health facilities, employment opportunities, free education, and social welfare programs, as well as other local community development programs, empower the enslaveables through the provision of preventive measures. These measures reduce the enslaveables' vulnerability and empower them, depending on the availability and effectiveness of such ancillary sources. These sources also provide viable ex-post alternatives for MDS victims, and their families, as protective screens against MDS practices. Effective alternative options reduce the enslavement rent by reducing the enslaveables' vulnerability, and provide viable alternatives to MDS victims and their families.

Studies show that globalization and international trade are not likely to increase the incidence of child labor or MDS practices, since they offer employment opportunities to adults, especially women, and are subject to more scrutiny and international labor codes of conduct (Dean, 2005). Recent studies show that greater market integration in LDCs is associated with less child labor. Moreover, studies show that children living in or around cities work much less, in total, than their rural counterparts, with higher school attendance rates. Generally, urban proximity is associated with an overall improvement in child welfare (Fafchamps and Wahba, 2006, p. 2). These factors explain the important role of alternative sources, such as adult employment, adequate schooling for children, and internal mobility, in reducing the vulnerability of the enslaveables.

A lack of second sources eliminates the enslaveables' options regarding better transactions and terms, and makes them more vulnerable to MDS schemes. For example, even though children have the right to go to school, no functioning schools exist, especially in various rural and poor areas in India, due to corrupt local governments there. Even though the enslaveables (e.g., SC/ST in India) have formal rights under the constitution, ineffective enforcement of the law and the lack of programs aimed at increasing the enslaveables' human capital (e.g., education and health), social capital (e.g., social networks), economic empowerment, and employment opportunities, repress these formal rights and restrict their effects.[70] The enslaveables' ignorance (or unawareness) of existing laws and procedures, excessive delays and insensitivity of the judicial systems towards them, and the inability of the enslaveables to afford the cost of obtaining justice, contribute to the enslaveables' continued vulnerability (Human Rights Watch, 1999, p. 175). The lack of viable second sources takes away the enslaveables' capabilities to choose, and degrades them to mere adjuncts of the communities in which they live, whose mission is to execute the plans of someone else (e.g., upper-caste members or MDS perpetrators) (Nussbaum, 2000, pp. 54-56; UNICEF, 2004, p. 17). The powerlessness and vulnerability of the poor and the arbitrary actions of those in power can be seen in a recent example from India. In 2005 and 2006, after the police and labor officials – with the help of child-rights NGOs – freed about 500 children, between 6-12 years of age, from sweatshops across Delhi, the Delhi government failed to rehabilitate them; for a week, the police locked the children in an empty shopping mall that was used as a temporary shelter for beggars. Later, they were sent to observation homes used primarily for juvenile delinquents, without any real attempt to address these

---

[70] The Asian Centre for Human Rights reports incidences of misuse of funds allocated for SC/ST development projects, the failure to fill thousands of backlogged posts reserved for SC/ST in many states in India, the denial of SC/ST's access to land, resources, and their right to franchise, and their access to schools (Chakma, 2007).

children's root problems, such as severe poverty, family debts, marginalization, and migration of their parents (Gentleman, 2006; Chopra, 2006; Chakma, 2007, p. 54). In another instance, after dance bars in Maharashtra State were closed, the lack of second sources (including rehabilitation) forced those women employed there into prostitution in other cities/destinations (U.S. DOS, 2005a, Section 5).

The perpetrators, taking full advantage of their superior information and the lack of effective second sources, normally expose the enslaveables to take-it-or-leave-it offers, designed to serve the perpetrators' interests at the expense of the MDS victims. The victims' rights and perpetrators' liabilities are intentionally not documented in such transactions, which, in turn, enables the perpetrators to secure all the transactions they desire, leaving the enslaveables and the victims unable to secure anything.

Much in contrast to the victims' possibilities, MDS perpetrators do have access to second sources and are able to take advantage of them. For examples, the perpetrators are able to move their practices from one place or sector to another to avoid potential intervention or prosecution by governments and other NGOs. They also have the resources and power to leverage the collaboration of corrupt officials who share part of the enslavement rent.

2.9 Property rights

A unique attribute of MDS practices is that the MDS victims become the objects of the transactions, rather than being negotiators or active participants. The lack of, or incomplete property rights – in terms of definitions, structures, boundaries, and enforcement – makes it easier for the MDS perpetrators to extract more enslavement rent at the expense of the enslaved and enslaveables.

In extreme instances, the perpetrators can transform the enslaveables into objects that can be exchanged like other tradable commodities; the victims lose the rights to their most intrinsic properties – their time, energy, bodies, and, in extreme cases, their lives.

The peculiar aspect of property rights in modern-day slavery is the perpetrators' rights over their victims; the more right the perpetrators have, or can exercise on MDS victims, the higher their share of the enslavement rent, at the expense of MDS victims.

The following examples illustrate the utter cruelty of such practices. First, in India, young girls, generally from the SC/ST, are taken from their families and given to a Hindu priest or temple as "servants of God" or "*Devadasis.*" These prepubescent girls are required to provide sexual services to priests (U.S. DOS, 2003a, Section 6c). Second, the rights to a woman, in some states in India, are transferred to the husband's family at the time of marriage (Das Gupta and Shuzhuo, 1999). Third, the prevalence of female infanticide in India, which takes place before the registration of the newborn, sends a clear signal of the devalued status of women in India.[71] Fourth, MDS perpetrators' purchase infant females (one to two years old) from their families for adoption, in order to train these infants for the sex trade, pornography, and, later on, to sell them again into the sex industry when they are seven to twelve years old. Lastly, children of impoverished families, mostly SC/ST, were sold into an organized ring at the annual Sonepur cattle fair in Bihar, India, for the purpose of domestic labor and forced sexual services (U.S. DOS, 2000a, Section 6c).

2.10 The signaling effect

The signaling effect plays a significant role in the practice and perpetuation of modern-day slavery in LDCs. Many MDS practices are initiated

---

[71] The practices of female feticide and infanticide are still widespread in India, especially in rural areas, according to human rights groups' estimates. The national ratio of female to male in the population is about 927 females per 1000 males. In some districts in Haryana and Punjab, the gender population gap is so severe that the ratio of females to males is lower than 80% (U.S. DOS, 2007a, Section 5).

through false signals from MDS perpetrators to the enslaveables. For example, loans and cash advances that accompany promises of employment or marriage, paid by the MDS perpetrator to the enslaveables, send a false signal of credibility regarding the MDS perpetrators' offers, and can trap the enslaveables into accepting binding MDS transactions with the MDS perpetrators.

Governments and their agencies, which are obliged to abide by human rights conventions and laws, may send implicit signals to perpetrators to continue their practices, through the ineffective enforcement of such laws. In many cases, legal and political interventions fall short of enforcing the laws, in terms of prosecuting the perpetrators, or rescuing and protecting MDS victims.[72] Examples of such ineffective MDS law enforcement include dismal prosecution records, accompanied by very low conviction rates,[73] the prevalence of bribery (often leading to the immediate release of MDS perpetrators or the imposition of negligible fines against them), and the government's apathy regarding rescuing and protecting the victims. In essence, it becomes a legal system that prosecutes the enslaved instead of the perpetrators.[74] Corrupt government officials and police

---

[72] Enforcement of the Bonded Labour System (Abolition) Act of 1976 in India, which is the responsibility of state and local governments, varies among states. It has not been effective, due to inadequate resources and social acceptances of bonded/forced labor. Additionally, the role of India's National Human Right Commission (NHRC) to supervise states' implementation of bonded labor laws, as ordered by India's Supreme Court in 1997, is limited, due to the NHRC's limited resources and power and because it is not a law enforcement agency (Human Rights Watch, 2003). Lack of coordination between police and NGOs resulted in ineffective raids; thus, worsening the situation of girls and women indebted to traffickers and brothel owners (U.S. DOS, 2002a, Section 6f). According to this act, payments lower than minimum wage, for the purpose of paying debt, are considered bonded labor.

[73] Similarly, between 1997 and 2002, the state of Tamil Nadu initiated only 100 prosecutions in response to 37,082 identified cases of bonded labor. Furthermore, most of these 100 cases ended in acquittal (Human Right Watch, 2003). In 2005, the conviction rate for crimes against the Dalits was 3.9% in the State of Gujarat, 5.9% in the State of Maharashtra, and 8% in the State of Kerala (Chakma, 2006).

[74] NGOs — knowing about the trafficking of women and children in brothel areas, the traffickers, and the locations of the brothels — were reluctant to trust the police with such information, based on past records of arresting the victims, instead of rescuing them (U.S. DOS, 2002a, Section 6f).

also harass, intimidate, and sometimes attack NGOs and human rights agents.[75] According to Human Rights Watch (1999, pp. 23-24), the Indian government's interventions to grant certain reservations to SC/ST in education, government jobs, and government bodies, have benefited very few and have had little effect, due to the government's lack of political will. Recent reports show the government's failure to fill over 50,000 vacant positions reserved for SC/ST (U.S. DOS, 2006a, Section 5).

In addition, excessive punishments and credible threats by MDS perpetrators against the victims (and their families), send clear signals to the victims and their families to submit to the perpetrators' orders, and deter them from seeking government interventions,[76] especially in the case of corrupt or collaborating officials. Furthermore, according to NGOs' reports, 80-90 percent of the arrests made under the ITPA (Immoral Trafficking Prevention Act) were of female sex workers (many of them forced sex workers or MDS victims). In addition, the reports note the very poor records of rehabilitation and protection of rescued victims, until recently.[77] Only a small fraction of the arrests involved

---

[75] According to Human Rights Watch's 2003 World Report on India, police obstructed NGOs attempts to deliver supplies to relief camps. Other agents were subjected to attacks, with reports of death. Such harassment and intimidation were extended against international NGOs as well. The Asian Centre for Human Rights (ACHR) reported, in April 2004, such harassment by local authorities, including the denials of government services, and intimidating visits from security forces/police, especially in local areas. However, the U.S. Department of State also reports instances where many other domestic and international NGOs do operate without government restriction (U.S. DOS, 2006a, Section 4). Intimidation and harassment have occurred in a few circumstances.

[76] Human Rights Watch (2003) recorded the violence and attacks by Hindu upper castes against the enslaveables (SC/ST). These attacks were conducted to heighten the enslaveables' vulnerability, by destroying their assets and belongings. Caste violence against SC/ST has increased in recent years, costing hundreds of lives, according to human rights NGOs' reports, especially in certain states such as Pradesh, Bihar, Rajasthan, Madhya Pradesh, Tamil Nadu, and Andhra Pradesh. Such violence covers the entire spectrum of social, economic, and political activities, both individually and collectively (U.S. DOS, 2006a, Section 5).

[77] The police no longer arrest trafficked women and children for soliciting in larger cities, such as Delhi, Bangalore, and Mumbai, and such arrests have diminished in other states. In addition, the ITPA requires female officers to interrogate girls rescued from brothels. The Indian government also has increased police training and the number of shelters available to rescued victims (U.S. DOS, 2005a, Section 5).

traffickers (U.S. DOS, 2005a, Section 5). Such signals influence the mental imagery (to interpret the surrounding environment) of MDS victims and perpetrators in opposite ways, based on their learning from the outcomes that are consistent or inconsistent with their expectations (North, 1998). The above signals are likely to make the victims surrender to MDS practices, and encourage the perpetrators to continue such practices, thereby reducing the risks associated with MDS industries and increasing the perpetrators' share of the enslavement rent, ultimately protecting and perpetuating MDS practices.

The poor conditions associated with a career in law enforcement (e.g., low pay, inadequate housing, long work hours) contribute to police corruption and, therefore, the ineffective enforcement of the law. Often police officers seek the protection of an underworld figure, or "Godfather," simply to survive. According to the National Police Commission's 1980 report, police abuses specific to the SC/ST include: police refusal to register SC/ST's complaints; half-hearted actions; extreme brutality in dealing with accused SC/ST (or weaker sections); soft treatment of accused Caste members (or influential sections); and arresting SC/ST or failing to arrest Caste Hindus on mala fide considerations (Human Rights Watch, 1999, pp. 32-33; Chakma, 2007).

On the contrary, effective enforcement of existing laws, in terms of prosecuting MDS perpetrators, freeing the victims, and implementing programs to protect and empower the enslaveables, reduces the vulnerability and desperation of the enslaveables and increases the costs and risks associated with MDS practices. This, in turn, reduces the expected net enslavement rent, and, therefore, diminishes or eliminates MDS practices.[78] The presence and cooperation among

[78] India's Supreme Court decision, in 1996, is a good example of effective interventions that punish the perpetrators and help the victims. The Court ordered states to identify children who are employed illegally, remove the children, fine the employer, and deposit the fine in a rehabilitation-cum-welfare fund to rehabilitate the victim, employ an adult family member, and to prosecute the employers. In 1997, the Court ordered states to gradually provide compulsory primary education to all children employed in factories, either by the industries themselves or with

NGOs, as effective second sources, and interest groups that act against MDS practices and support MDS victims and the enslaveables send strong signals against MDS practices.[79]

2.11 Double/multiple entrapments

The double-trap effect refers to the perpetrators' pre-emptive tactics to heighten the victims' vulnerability, which, in turn, boosts the perpetrators' shares of enslavement rent. For example, confiscating the victims' legal documents, especially in the cases of cross-country trafficking of MDS victims, and involving the victims in illegal acts, or acts that the victims perceive to be illegal, entraps the victims twice, due to their actual or perceived illegal status and their fear of prosecution. Consequently, victims may not be able to complain, resist, escape, or report MDS practices; their options become limited to either being enslaved or attempt escape and expose themselves to legal prosecution (a Catch 22!). Examples of laws broken by MDS victims include: the victims' unlawful entry into the country by the perpetrators (trafficking); lack of legal documentation, (confiscated or destroyed by the perpetrators); and participation in illegal practices such as prostitution, which is forced on them by the perpetrators.[80] Such traps transform MDS victims into hunted (actual or perceived) criminals. As stated in the 2002 Report on Human Rights Practices in India, "Victims of

---

coordination with state governments, in addition to heath check-ups and nutritious food (Human Rights Watch, 2003).

[79] *Navsarjan,* an NGO that campaigned to abolish manual scavenging in the State of Gujarat, India, is an example of an NGO that attempts to empower the SC/ST through alternative employment and rehabilitation of those scavengers who are worthy of performing better jobs (although scavengers are convinced that they are destined to scavenge). *Safai Karmachari Andolan,* is another example of an NGO, in the state of Andhra Pradesh, India, which disseminates information about scavenging and MDS practices (Human Rights Watch, 1999, pp. 141-42).

[80] Section 8 of the Immoral Trafficking Prevention Act (ITPA), in India, is an example of a Catch 22. It criminalizes the act of solicitation for prostitution, which is used to arrest and punish the forced sex worker (MDS victim); some of them are victims of domestic and international trafficking (U.S. DOS, 2005b, Section V).

trafficking were subject to threats, including emotional blackmail, violence, and confinement, as well as the threat of apprehension by authorities, detention, prosecution and deportation" (U.S. DOS, 2002a, Section 6f). The fate of former *Devadasis*, who are auctioned as forced prostitutes and sold to brothels, is another example of a double-trap: existing laws may criminalize the former *Devadasis* (as forced prostitutes) instead of the MDS perpetrators (brothels' owners/patrons), if these former *Devadasis* report such MDS practices to police.[81]

A successful double-trap effect can sustain MDS practices for as long as the victims' fear of prosecution prevents them from escaping or reporting such practices. Perpetrators utilize the double-trap effect by pretending to protect the victims from prosecution, or by threatening to report the victims' 'illegal' activities to authorities, which, in turn, helps perpetuate MDS practices, as the 'lesser of two evils.'

2.12 The collective marginalization of enslaveables

The marginalization effect refers to the outcome of social disconnection of a certain population group (or groups) based on certain attributes that are embedded in informal norms, traditions, and religious beliefs, so these certain population groups become condemned, marginalized, and considered "inferior" by society, or other influential groups. The marginalization effect transforms such "inferior" groups into social outcasts, making them vulnerable to harassment and discriminating practices, such as modern-day slavery – especially when sanctioned by judicial injunctions against these marginalized groups. As Péter Bauer (1981) stated so well: "The poorest and most backward people have few or no external contacts; witness the aborigines, pygmies and desert peoples" (p. 70).

---

[81] Even though the state of Karnataka, India, passed the Karnataka *Devadasi* (Prohibition of Dedication) Act in 1992, the enforcement of such an act is ineffective; police corruption and collaboration with brothels' owners, and police sexual abuse of the former *Devadasis* were common (Human Rights Watch, 1999, pp. 150-52).

Marcel Fafchamps (2004) also underscores the influence of cultural norms: "In stable pre-industrial economics, exchange may be influenced by culturally inherited economic roles" (p. 20). Moreover, customs, and the adherence to them, play significant roles in perpetuating the marginalization of certain groups, e.g., SC/ST in India, in which the society is divided into mutually exclusive groups (castes), with members of these castes adhering to preset codes of behavior. Members who do not follow such codes will be outcast (Akerlof, 1976, p. 610). Furthermore, all other members should treat the violators as outcaste; otherwise, they will be outcast, too. Such rigid and exclusive practices perpetuate the marginability of the low castes and outcastes. For examples, the outcastes are permitted to hold only scavenging or other desecrated jobs; they are not allowed to eat with caste members, touch their food, touch them, and their children will also be outcastes (Akerlof, 1976, p. 610; Saintsbury, 1972). According to Akerlof (1976), if the punishment for becoming an outcaste is predicted to be sufficiently severe, the caste system will be sustained (p. 610). In such a rigid system, no individual, merely by behaving differently, can improve his/her social standing – except for those already at the lowest ranking (low castes or outcastes), where social punishments should not matter to them since they are already at the bottom of the social ranking. The only types of punishment that can continue to work are coercive punishments such as physical harm or kidnapping of MDS victims (p. 611). Consequently, the winners of such a societal structure are not likely to change their behaviors, while, the marginalized and lowest-ranked groups must necessarily evaluate the benefit and costs of their behaviors: if they obey such discriminatory societal rules, they will accept and sustain their marginalized and vulnerable status. Yet, if they defy these rules, they will expose themselves to coercive punishment. A third option may arise, which is for the marginalized group (low castes and outcastes) to abandon their discriminating community and move/migrate to communities that do not apply such discriminatory rules.

However, this option can be very costly and difficult, financially and socially, especially in collectivist communities.

If the punishment of becoming an outcaste is predicted to be sufficiently severe, the predictions of the caste system become a self-fulfilling prophecy.[82]

The above analysis applies to other societies and communities that have similar societal structures associated with exclusive groups, especially in poor collectivist communities. The *Dinka*, and other indigenous tribes in Sudan, the *Black Moors*, and other southerners in Mauritania (U.S. DOS, 2004c and 2004d), and Thai females, who are considered impure, carnal, and corrupt, according to certain Buddhist beliefs are all vulnerable to MDS practices, as well (Bales, 1999; De Bary, 1998; Lim, 1998; Sawyer, 1986).

The marginalization effect also highlights the limitation of focusing on short-term interventions such as freeing MDS victims and prosecuting MDS perpetrators which do not eliminate the causes of marginalization. It emphasizes the significance of long-term interventions that do work to gradually transform such embedded discriminatory informal norms and practices and consequently eliminate the built-in marginalization of certain groups of the population.

2.13 Status or positional goods

Status or positional goods confer utility to someone (a certain group) only at the expense of someone else (or another group) who consumes less of the status good. Hirsch (1976) distinguishes between 'normal goods,' which confer direct utility (yielding a positive sum game in free market transactions, where everyone can gain), and 'positional goods' (which confer utility to some at the expense of others (a zero- or a negative-sum-game) (Cooper, et al., 2001, p. 642). Material goods are reproducible, but positional or status goods are not. As individuals (or

---

[82] In this case, the system of caste (or similar discriminating societal structures) will be held in equilibrium, irrespective of individual preference or taste. For further detail see Akerlof (1976, p. 610)

groups) compete for the fixed supply of positional goods, they (or at least some of them) become frustrated (ibid, p. 643). "Like Hirsch's positional goods, status goods confer utility only at the expense of someone who consumes less of the good" (ibid, p. 644).

Examples of status goods that are relevant to the understanding of modern-day slavery in LDCs include decisions concerning employment (e.g., types of jobs imposed on the SC/ST in India), and political and social representations. The inherited skewed distribution of status goods in many communities in LDCs highlights the perpetuation of MDS practices there. The improvement of the wellbeing (or utility or welfare) that accrues to a certain population group (e.g., the elite and upper-caste population) must take place at the expense of another (e.g., the enslaveables and lower-caste population).

The enslaveables' lack of status goods reduces their resistance to MDS practices. It is also likely to reduce the effectiveness of interventions against MDS practices (into transitory effects), which does not last without improving the status of the enslaveables (or enhancing the enslaveables holding of status goods). This can only be achieved by redistributing the status goods from the elite and upper-caste population groups, including MDS perpetrators.

2.14 Cognitive dissonance

Cognitive dissonance plays a vital role in perpetuating certain practices that may seem irrational. People who are subject to discrimination, e.g., the enslaveables and MDS victims, are likely to become oblivious to such discrimination. They are likely to minimize and justify the discrimination against them, such that they make themselves feel less discriminated against, especially if there is no way out, or if the cost of rebelling is very high or prohibitive. Their apparent acceptance of such discriminating norms and practices should not be considered as the last word on the matter (Nussbaum, 2000, p. 43). They understand that if they resist or complain, they will face harsh punishments. Accordingly, the enslaveables and MDS victims may even resist intervention.

Furthermore, there are discriminations and MDS practices that are exploited by higher-level SC/ST against lower-level SC/ST. This explains the multiple layers of MDS practices, such that the internally higher-level SC/ST can copy the upper castes behavior, in exploiting the vulnerability and enslaveablity of lower-level SC/ST (U.S. DOS, 2006a, Section 5).

"A great deal of anecdotal information suggests that workers in dangerous jobs are often quite oblivious to the dangers that are involved" (Akerlof and Dickens, 1982, p. 307). People in collectivist societies who are subject to discrimination may follow the same concept; they become oblivious to the dangers that are involved. "Analysis that takes account of cognitive dissonance gives different results from the standard analysis, and in particular, provides better explanations for some phenomena that are a puzzle according to the standard approach"(Akerlof and Dickens, 1982, p. 318).

The enslaveables and MDS victims are likely to be reluctant to report incidents of MDS practices and discrimination to police and government because of their fear of police abuse and refusal to register the Dalits' complaints against higher-caste Hindus. Police, mostly from higher-caste Hindus, typically refuse to enforce legislations that protect Dalits, and they usually are subject to the influence of the landlords and upper-caste politicians (Human Rights Watch, 1999, p. 23). The vulnerable groups, e.g., SC/ST, are likely to behave as if their situation is less dangerous or stressful, and that they are treated fairly, according the collectivist informal codes of conduct. They have a choice about their beliefs. People with strong beliefs in informal norms (e.g., codes of conduct, taboos, myths, religious constraints) are more likely to have persistent belief that the undertaking is a good one. Nussbaum (2000, p. 114) referred to the idea of preference deformation, where unjust norms, traditions, fear, and discriminating cultural and social backgrounds can deform people's preferences, choices, and even wishes for their own lives. Moreover, MDS perpetrators will continue their

MDS practices with the expectation that they will not be caught, especially if the corrupt institutional environment supports their belief that in legal community or that they will be treated less harshly if apprehended.

This issue lends great importance to external interventions; since well-established internal institutions are less likely to change from within, and may need the injection of outside reformative measures to produce viable long-lasting changes.

In the terminology of social psychology, cognitive dissonance represents the conflicting desires that create an unpleasant tension. The cognitive dissonance theory proposes that people are motivated to reduce this tension and may, in this context, do so either by reducing self-interested behavior, or by engaging in self-deception, or by some combination of the two (Konow, 2000, p. 1073).[83]

Typically, people would not choose to work in an unsafe place, but if they do continued to work in dangerous jobs, they would try to reject the cognition that the job is dangerous. This behavior is crucial to the understanding of appalling phenomena such as modern-day slavery, since the enslaveable and MDS victims may not iden

tify themselves as victims. Their measurement of victimization may have been corrupted. Thus, external intervention is vital. First, it identifies victims who may fail to identify themselves as victims, and second, since these victims may not initiate any intervention on their own, it is necessary for external actors to identify them as victims.[84] Akerlof and Dickens (1982) state this clearly: "Persons

---

[83] One example of cognitive dissonance is the failure or indifference of persons with high risk of flood or earthquake damage to purchase flood or earthquake insurance since they believe that their work/home is safe (Akerlof and Dickens, 1982, p. 308). This corresponds to the premise that people have preferences over their beliefs, and that they can control their beliefs by selecting certain information and decisions that align with their desired belief (pp. 307-308). Accordingly, the enslaveables and MDS victims typically believe that their situation is safe (or less dire), and that they are treated fairly, according to the existing collectivist informal norms and codes of conduct.

[84] For more examples and studies on cognitive dissonance, see Knox and Inkster (1968), Brehm (1956), and Kunreuther et al. (1978).

tend to avoid or resist new information that contradicts already established beliefs" (p. 316). People with strong belief in informal norms (e.g., codes of conduct, taboos, myths, religious constraints) are more likely to believe that the undertaking of difficult or unpleasant tasks is good (ibid, p. 310). The enslaveables may thus tend to believe that they will fare better in dealing with MDS perpetrators, hoping for the best to happen. This of course plays right into the hands of the MDS perpetrators.[85]

2.15 Social capital

"Social capital" is the name given to a store of value generated when a group of individuals invests resources in fostering a body of relationships with each other (a "social network"). These relationships, it is argued, create trust by fostering shared norms, improve contract enforcement by easing information flows, and enhance sanctions against deviant behavior by facilitating collective action. This is held to benefit the entire society. (Ogilvie, 2004, Paragraph 3)

Social capital helps to explain the characteristics of certain institutions that facilitate discrimination against marginalized population groups (e.g., the enslaveables). Social networks generate beneficial social capital such as information transformation, norm enforcements, and collective actions. These social networks have a distributional affect that harms the interest of the network outsiders (e.g., the marginalized and enslaveables), and leads to investment and accumulation of social capital for the network insiders (e.g., the elite and upper castes). Accordingly, exploiting social capital can serve as another form of rent-seeking practices.

---

[85] This thought was first expressed by Akerlof and Dickens (1982), "people may want to believe that what they have just bought meets their needs. Advertising gives people some external justification for believing just that. People like to feel that they are attractive, socially adept, and intelligent. It makes them feel good to hold such beliefs – if the person buys the advertised product" (p. 317).

Ogilvie (2004) identifies the following two types of social networks that generate social capital. First, "*closure* means that network membership is clearly and finitely defined, increasing the density of interactions between members and thereby intensifying the quality and reliability of the information sharing and third-party monitoring needed to enforce cooperation" (Paragraph 13). Closure helps to generate social capital that benefits network members. However, such network based social capital harms outsiders, such as the marginalized and the enslaveables, and can harm the entire economy and society through cronyism, limited trade, and social conflict. The second type of social networks is the, *multiplex relationships* that help create social capital by expanding the means available to members of a social network who interact in multiple spheres (e.g., economic, religious, social, and political), "punishing deviance in, and urging collective action on one another" (Paragraph 14).

The lack of social capital diminishes the effectiveness of development programs in poor communities. Low-caste people, especially in rural regions, are not necessarily helped by community development programs that reinforce the advantages of the higher castes. Studies show the predominance of benefits given to the elite under community development programs in rural India, where the poor are alienated by such governmental programs, which are manipulated by the local elite (high castes) who dominate local councils (Berreman, 1966, pp. 91-92). When the elite control community development programs, they will oppose any government intervention that changes the social structures, especially in rural areas.

The enslaveables' position on status goods depends on their access to and their accumulation of social capital. Their lack of social capital, due to their exclusion from effective social networks and/or multiplex relationships, reduces their position of status goods.[86] The untouchability practices in the Hindu-caste

---

[86] See Human Rights Watch (1999, Chapter III) for examples of imposing social disabilities, and exclusive practices against SC/ST, by the Hindu-caste system.

system impose social disabilities on the enslaveables because of exclusive practices against the SC/ST, especially where the SC/ST are a minority. Social boycotts and retaliatory acts are used against SC/ST who attempt to defy the caste social order (Human Rights Watch, 1999, p. 26). In addition, there exists pre-market discrimination against the vulnerable and enslaveables that prohibits them from engaging in certain jobs (reserved for upper castes), and imposes certain menial jobs on them. Pre-market discrimination intensifies the enslaveables' vulnerability and needs, such that they become vulnerable to MDS perpetrators' schemes.

Ogilvie (2004) explains the negative effect of social networks on non-members in Europe in the seventeenth century, and on society over all. "Formal-sector social networks such as guilds, by using their social capital to force non-members into the 'informal sector,' harm not just the outsiders who are prevented from earning a legal living but also the economy as a whole" (Paragraph 30). Violations were met with strict punishments. These social networks force the non-members into black markets (the informal sector), and the enslaveables into becoming victims of MDS schemes/practices, even in the twenty-first century, in some LDCs. Such social prejudices cause the enslaveables to underinvest in human capital such as education and training, which, in turn, deepens their vulnerability and perpetuates their second-class status (Nussbaum, 2002, pp. 116-117; Becker, 1995, p. 634).

The high density of multiplex relationships among the same caste or social class that results when caste members also share the same religious practices and other multi-standard relationships helps to generate the social capital of common norms, shared information, and collective sanctions (Ogilvie, 2004, Paragraph 34). Accumulating social capital widens the gap between the holders of social capital and the others (non-members, including the enslaveables and other vulnerable groups). Such skewed distribution of social capital harms the vulnerable groups in terms of excluding them from specific decision-making processes, such as access to common resources, certain jobs, where to live, ownership and/or inheritance of assets, or even recognizing them as full members of the communities, etc. Community councils may enhance such distributive effect of accumulating social capital by favoring the members of social network and multiplex-relationships, and imposing sanctions on non-members or designated groups – for example, the enslaveables.

Finally, even though the enslaveables may have social networks among themselves, they are prevented from generating significant social capital (Ogilvie, 2004, Paragraph 57).

Chapter 4

Interventions, Remedies, and Cautions

This is what the LORD says: Do what is just and right. Rescue from the hand of his oppressor the one who has been robbed. Do no wrong or violence to the alien, the fatherless or the widow, and do not shed innocent blood in this place. (Jeremiah 22:3)

[...] I swore never to be silent whenever wherever human beings endure suffering and humiliation. We must take sides. Neutrality helps the oppressor, never the victim. Silence encourages the tormentor, never the tormented. Sometimes we must interfere. When human lives are endangered, when human dignity is in jeopardy, national borders and sensitivities become irrelevant. Wherever men and women are persecuted because of their race, religion, or political views, that place must – at that moment – become the center of the universe. Elie Wiesel (1986, Paragraph 10)

In general, people seek not the way of their ancestors, but the good. Aristotle, Politics, 1269a, pp. 3-4.

The complexity of MDS practices requires coordinated multi-level, multifaceted interventions over short, medium, and long term time horizons that address the roots, causes, and symptoms of these practices. Intervention should also alter the behavior and the capabilities of the different participating groups, from MDS victims to MDS perpetrators. Furthermore, interventions should recognize and engage the different layers of MDS practices, from local to international.

Section 1 highlights the scope of the intervention, in terms of timeline (immediate, short-term, intermediate-term, and long-term), and the different levels of intervention (local, national, and international). Section 2 highlights special considerations for effective interventions.

1. Scope of Intervention and Remedies

Effective intervention and remedies to modern-day slavery must include built-in mechanisms that respond to MDS practices from their roots to their final symptoms. New institutional economic analysis of modern-day slavery draws special attention to the importance of timeline intervention and remedies.

The main objective of the proposed interventions and remedies is to minimize the enslavement rent – the major drive behind MDS practices. Thus, interventions should be evaluated in terms of their effectiveness in reducing the enslavement rent, rescuing MDS victims, minimizing the vulnerability of the enslaveables, and empowering them. Such interventions should increase the perpetrators' costs and risks as well.

Consequently, interventions and remedies should be comprehensive with regard to timeline (immediate/very-short-term, short-term, medium-term, and long-term), levels of interventions (local, national, and international), and agents of interventions (government, non-government, and civil-society organizations).

The discriminating environment against enslaveables is so complex that it has penetrated almost all aspects of their lives. As a result, fixing one problem may destabilize the existing balance and may generate more unwanted ramifications. What can be done? First, there is an urgent need to decipher such a complex cobweb of discriminating environments, and separate the levels of institutions that may shed more light on the root causes/symptoms of such discrimination. Then, intervention should be customized to engage these root causes, instead of focusing, falsely, on the symptoms of such discriminating environments.

1.1 Intervention timeline

Effective intervention should address and respond to time-based roots, causes, and symptoms of modern-day slavery. The following four phases address and respond to the time-sensitive institutional mechanism. Immediate interventions aim to free existing MDS victims; short-term interventions aim to reduce the enslaveables' vulnerability; intermediate-term interventions aim to empower the enslaveables; and long-term interventions aim to reverse the embedded cultural norms and traditions that instigate and perpetuate modern-day slavery.

Proper timeline intervention should take into consideration the particular objectives and constraints that are linked to each of the following four phases of intervention: immediate, short-term, medium-term, and long-term.

1.1.1 Immediate or very-short-term interventions and remedies

Immediate and short-term interventions respond with urgency to the dire status of actual MDS victims. Rescuing and releasing these victims should be the first and immediate step of intervention.[87]

Other support and relief programs should accompany and follow the immediate release of these victims, prompting the next phase: short-term intervention, which aims at reducing the vulnerability levels of the enslaveables.[88] Effective presence and inspection by governmental and non-governmental agencies, such as human rights and civil-society organizations, should deter and preempt any attempt to re-enslave these former victims.[89]

---

[87] In a surprise inspection by a Human Rights Watch (HRW) team, headed by the Karnataka State Labor Commissioner, of silk twining factories in and around the town of Magadi, India, there were 3000 cases of bonded child laborers in the Magadi silk twining factories. UNICEF, in 1998, started an informal education program for these 3000 children, and provided their parents with a micro-credit program to create alternative income-generating opportunities (U.S. DOS, 2000a, and 2003a). Raiding suspected factories and freeing children has had some success, though. In one raid, 28 children were freed; four of them had been kidnapped (Jacobs, 1996).

[88] The National Child Labor Project (NCLP), India began, in 1998, releasing children from hazardous workplaces and providing them with transitional schooling, which has resulted in mainstreaming in regular schools. Between April 1999 and January 2000, 145,725 children participated in the NCLP. More than 500,000 have been helped since its inception. It also pays the participating children's families a stipend of $2.15 to $4.30 (100 to 200 rupees) per month to compensate for the loss of their children's income (U.S. DOS, 2000a).

[89] The Union Ministry of Social Justice and Empowerment, India, has set up a 24-hour 'child help line' phone-in service in nine cities for children in distress. They are run by NGOs with government funding. The help lines received 25,000 calls in a six-month period (U.S. DOS, 2001a, Section 5).

1.1.2 Short-term interventions and remedies

The main goal of this phase is to reduce the vulnerability and neediness of the enslaveables and former MDS victims, through the provision of basic human needs (food, shelter, clothing, water and sanitation, and education), protection and security. These provisions must be accompanied by the visibility and actual presence of intervening agents (to deter further attempts by MDS perpetrators), and informing the enslaveables about their legal rights, according to the current practices of laws.

Effective interventions should also pursue the prosecution and punishment of MDS perpetrators and their collaborators, through imprisonment and large penalties.[90] Investigating and providing evidence of violations of existing laws should deter further MDS practices and increase the costs and risks of such practices.[91] The surrounding social and power structure may support or hinder such intervention, depending on the level of intervention, government role, and the presence and interest of collaborators. Gathering information from former MDS victims seems vital to making such interventions effective.

Effective intervention should also aim to raise the enslaveables' information base regarding the presence of 'second sources' and other government programs such as micro-enterprise lending, vocational training, and rehabilitation and counseling programs. Furthermore, it should offer free and compulsory primary education for children in poor and marginalized regions, supported by free meals and school supplies, such as book and uniforms, which the very poor and the enslaveables cannot afford to buy on their own. Such direct

---

[90] A 1996 India Supreme Court decision raised the penalty for employers of children in hazardous industries to $430 (20,000 rupees) for each child employed, and established a welfare fund for formerly employed children.

[91] According to the South Asian Coalition on Child Servitude (SACCS), authorities are pursuing some 6000 cases against employers (U.S. DOS, 2000a, Section 6d).

government and non-government intervention can counterbalance the presence of cultural norms and traditions that discriminate against the enslaveables.[92]

The availability of information, per se, may have little effect on eliminating modern-day slavery. The crucial issue is disseminating and accommodating such information to the literacy and intellectual levels of MDS victims and the enslaveables. Effective dissemination of information to the enslaveables plays a crucial role in narrowing the information gap between them and the perpetrators, and, consequently, reducing the enslavement rent. The effective presence and visibility of support groups (e.g., agents of civil society and other NGOs at the local, national, and international levels) provides noticeable access and more efficient delivery, and dissemination, of such information to the enslaveables. Proper means of information delivery, such as cassette tapes and direct/verbal communications with the poor and marginalized, who are mostly illiterate, is also vital. The effective presence of second sources deters MDS practices by empowering the enslaveables, reducing their dependency on MDS perpetrators, and protecting them against illicit practices and rent seeking tactics used by MDS recruiters/ perpetrators.[93]

1.1.3 Medium-term interventions and remedies

The transition from short-term to medium-term interventions reflects the importance of empowering the former enslaveables in terms of gaining a social and political voice through active participation in the community and legislative

---

[92] A good example of such intervention is an experimentation scheme to combat gender discrimination, where the state government invests about $78, in the name of a newborn girl, into a saving account, to be given to her when she reaches the legal age of marriage, 18. The scheme is restricted to families with limited income and with no more than two children. The prime minister favors extending the plan to the entire country (The Economist, 1995a).

[93] The increased visibility of the National Human Rights Commission (NHRC, appointed by the Indian government in 1993) led to more complaints (40,724 between April 1998 and March 1999) of modern-day slavery and human rights violations (U.S. DOS, 2000a, Section 4).

bodies. The empowerment process should be accompanied by supporting social infrastructures, which contribute the most to upward mobility. These infrastructures include free and compulsory education, banking and loan services, accessible legal services, health clinics, employment and information offices, police stations and courts, participation in community development processes, and effective representation in legislative and political bodies and organizations. The equal distribution of the above services is key to economic justice (Walz-Chojnacki, 1999). Special arrangements should be offered to the former enslaveables to offset the presence of unjust cultural norms and traditions that still marginalize these groups.[94] Examples of these interventions include effective legislative representation (political quota) and special employment offers to the marginalized groups, who otherwise will be disconnected and ignored until the playing field is leveled.[95]

Interventions should seek effective enforcement of existing laws, fix any loopholes in those laws, and repeal existing unjust laws that perpetuate the abuse of vulnerable and marginalized groups.[96]

1.1.4 Long-term interventions and remedies

---

[94] The SC/ST, historically outside the caste system, are entitled, according to the Indian Constitution, to affirmative action and hiring quota in employment, special development funds, and training programs. In addition, the Scheduled Castes and Scheduled Tribes (Prevention of Atrocities) Act of 1989, and the Scheduled Castes and Schedules Tribes (Prevention of Atrocities) Rules, 1995, added new offenses, and provided stiffer penalties for offenders (U.S. DOS, 2000a, Section 5; Human Rights Watch, 1999, Appendix B).

[95] The "Panchayati Raj" constitutional amendments of 1993 reserved 30 percent of the seats in elected village councils (Panchayats) for women. This brought more than one million women into political life at the grassroots level (U.S. DOS, 2000a, Section 3c).

[96] The 1956 Suppression of Immoral Traffic Act (SITA) and the 1986 Immoral Trafficking Prevention Act (ITPA) intended to toughen penalties for trafficking in children, particularly on traffickers, pimps, landlords, and brothel operators, and to protect underage girls from becoming victims. They require the use of female police officers to interrogate girls rescued from brothels. They also grant quasi-toleration of prostitution, as prostitution, per se, is not a crime under the PITA, which criminalizes only solicitation, or practice, in or near a public place (U.S. DOS, 2000a and 2003a, Section 6f).

Cultures are dynamic and change is a very basic element in all of them.
Martha Nussbaum (2000, p. 48)

Long-term interventions should aim to reverse the course of unjust embedded informal norms and traditions (informal institutions) and repeal/change the unjust formal rules. Such ongoing processes could take decades or centuries. The gradual effect of such intervention requires the involvement of intervening agents and organizations that are willing to maintain their presence and exert the ongoing efforts required to modify, or repeal, these informal and formal institutions, hoping for a long-term correction. These agents and organizations must be equipped with a strong conviction and belief in the redemptive outcome of their intervention. These interventions should aim to level the playing field among the different population groups (winners and losers of existing informal norms and traditions) and reduce the divergence in their cultural heritages as a means of reducing the divergence in their mental models and perceptions (Denzau and North, 1993). Civil-society organizations and other NGOs may serve this cause better and more effectively than governments, since they are not constrained by the 'transitory' political gains or constraints that tend to reduce the participation of existing governmental agencies and organizations in such interventions.

Such interventions are more likely to face strong resistance from the privileged and powerful groups who gain from the presence of such norms/traditions.

Ongoing long-term interventions and remedies should also empower the poor, and develop marginalized communities (in order to level the playing field with other communities), through effective social and economic transformation, and continue the pressure to reverse existing unjust norms and traditions that contribute to the marginalization of the former enslaveables.

Long-term intervention should also take advantage of the built-in propensities to change found in embedded norms (e.g., *dharma*), which may be used to pursue changes in social and political institutions (Bondurant, 1966).

According to the Santi Parva, "In response to the demand of time and place what is proper may become improper and what is improper may become proper" (Bondurant 1966, p. 7).[97] NGOs and government agencies should also take advantage of the changes in cultural norms and practices in other societies to change public opinion and gain support for their goal: to transform the domestic cultural norms and traditions that perpetuate the social discrimination and the marginalization of certain population groups.

Studies show that economically successful caste members can adjust their social customs to reflect their social status, even in a caste-bound society such as India. Studies also show that economic success reduces taboos (Akerlof, 1976, p. 109; Srinivas, 1966, pp. 7-8; Lewis, 1965, pp. 70-77).

1.2 Levels of Intervention and Remedies

Effective intervention should take into consideration the specific characteristics, strengths, and limitations of intervention, at the local, national, and international levels.

1.2.1 Local intervention and remedies

Effective presence and visibility of community-based organizations (e.g., political, social, and religious), including local governments and NGOs, are crucial in dealing with locally-based MDS practices, since local governments and NGOs are more informed about the specifics of such practices in their districts and the surrounding areas. Effective local intervention utilizes such information to rescue the victims and to prosecute the perpetrators. Effective law enforcement against MDS practices and prosecution of MDS perpetrators, and the availability of viable second sources to the victims and the enslaveables (e.g., access to free education for children, welfare programs, employment, and credit facilities) are

---

[97] Translated from the Sanskrit by Ram Sharan Sharma in R. S. Sharma, Aspects of Political and Institution in Ancient India, Motilal Banarsidass, Delhi, 1959, p iii.

crucial, to reduce of the enslaveables' levels of desperation and vulnerability. The crucial role of intervention at the local level is clearly stated by members of the lowest Caste (Jatav) in Alipur, India: "Although the government has many good schemes, the officials in the middle eat it all... The government is making full effort to help the poor, but the officials don't allow any of the schemes to reach the poor," and "the police demand bribes and don't register complaints of scheduled caste people like me" (Gupta, 1995, p. 390). Such statements reflect how good intentions at the national and state levels can be frustrated by venal, local officials (such as police officers who demand bribes) (p. 391). NGO presence and interest in small/rural communities, especially in poor and marginalized regions such as slums and shantytowns, play a very significant role in helping the enslaveables and MDS victims there. Often, the marginalization of the enslaveables, and MDS practices at such local levels, typically do not attract or warrant government interventions at the national or state levels – especially with the lack of resources, competing interests, and prevalence of corruption. Therefore, NGOs' customized intervention is crucial. MDS practices, and marginalization of the enslaveables, are common, and frequently woven into the fabric of small and local communities, yet MDS practices typically do not reach a scale sufficient enough to attract the attention of government officials, and occasion the relocation of resources toward these poor and marginalized regions.

The effective presence of local NGOs, or the local presence of national and international NGOs and civil society organizations, and the collaboration between foreign NGOs and national and local NGOs in LDCs, play crucial roles against modern-day slavery, and other similar practices in LDCs (Hoksbergen, 2005). First, NGOs serve as viable second sources, rescuing and rehabilitating the enslaveables and MDS victims. NGOs increase the enslaveables' information base, provide social security nets (e.g., welfare programs, micro-enterprises, and loans to the enslaveables), train local officials regarding MDS practices and anti-

MDS laws and acts, and provide legal support and representation for the victims and the enslaveables. Second, they can participate in government interventions, in terms of reporting MDS practices, rescuing and rehabilitating MDS victims, and acting as watchdogs against MDS perpetrators. Third, NGOs can act as interest groups to ensure proper government interventions against MDS practices and perpetrators. Fourth, NGOs can establish strong relationships with honest and candid local leaders (e.g., police officers, judges, and public servants) to coordinate their efforts and resources to save MDS victims, reduce the vulnerability of the enslaveables and empower them, and prosecute MDS perpetrators (Haugen, 1999, P. 163). NGOs should utilize their effective influence as a specific kind of power (Basu 1986). The effective presence of NGOs in the enslaveables' communities gives NGOs direct access to information about MDS perpetrators' cheating behaviors. This information typically circulates freely among the enslaveables and helps NGOs to protect/help the enslaveables and to exclude the cheaters (MDS perpetrators) from future transactions with the enslaveables (Fafchamps, 2004, p. 201).

1.2.2 National intervention and remedies

Interventions at the national levels are more suited to the more complex and large-scale MDS practices and schemes such as prostitution and pedophilia rings, trafficking, and forced labor in exporting industries.

National governments' interventions are more effective in implementing national policies and programs dealing with formal rules (e.g., the Constitution, Penal Code, and numerous acts and commissions, in India). These policies prohibit MDS practices, protect the enslaveables, and empower them through national development programs, education and employment quota, and effective political representation for marginalized groups such as ethnic minorities (e.g.,

SC/ST) and women.[98] The vulnerability of women, children, and marginalized groups should be addressed through specific national programs such as compulsory and free primary education, employment opportunities, access to health clinics and micro-lending facilities programs, especially in poor and underdeveloped areas (meso-scale development programs).[99] For example, the National Policy on Education in India has provided special considerations for the education of the SC/ST (the Dalits). These considerations include:

1. Incorporating incentives for free textbooks, uniforms, and school bags for impoverished students

2. Building more primary schools within closer proximity to Dalit communities; abolition of tuition fees in government primary schools (with most states abolishing tuition for Dalit students through completion of the senior secondary levels)

3. Reserving certain seats for Dalits in the Central Government Institution of Higher Education

4. Special programs to improve the academic skills and linguistic proficiency for Dalit students

---

[98] The following articles from the Indian Constitution are of great relevance to preventing and eradicating MDS practices: Article 15 prohibits any discrimination based on religion, race, caste, sex or place of birth; Article 16 guarantees equal opportunity in public employment; Article 17 abolishes "Untouchability" in any form; Article 24 prohibits the employment of children in factories, mines, and other hazardous employment; Article 46 promotes the education and economic interests of SC/ST and other lower castes; and Article 243D (and articles 243T, 330, 332 , 334, and 335) offer affirmative action and reservation quota for SC/ST (Human Rights Watch, 1999, Appendix A).

[99] The new Indian government's Ministry of State for Women and Child Development has been welcomed as a positive step toward the eradication of sexual exploitation and the involuntary servitude that victimize vulnerable children and women in MDS industries. In addition, the Ministry is working to protect MDS victims' interests and to impose stricter penalties on MDS perpetrators, traffickers, and clients of such MDS practices (U.S. DOS, 2006b, Section VI).

5. Relaxing the scholarship requirements for Dalits and for their appointment to university lectureships.[100]

The reservation policy, which reserves a certain percentage of higher education and government jobs for the SC/ST, helps the SC/ST who face disadvantage in self-employment activities. These disadvantages stem from the existence of adverse informal norms against them (e.g., exclusive caste norms and employment practices) and their lack of social capital and productive assets, e.g., land (Unni, 2001, pp. 9-10, p. 25).[101]

Effective national governments' interventions, which deal with the enslaveables' persistent/chronic ultra-poverty, require larger transfers, and larger-scale programs, than those directed to other poor communities suffering from transitory poverty. This is due to the history-dependent social phenomena that explain the meso scale's poverty traps.[102] The enslaveables represent a meso group that suffers from chronic ultra-poverty by design, which, in turn, requires large-scale intervention to reduce their vulnerability and ultra-poverty. Small-transfers programs are likely to cause modest and transitory gains only, which may not be enough to escape poverty traps. The enslaveables are typically trapped into living in poor rural regions or in slums at the periphery of urban centers. They are typically landless, or own small marginal arable lands, far removed from markets and political centers, which usually attract low levels of government investments and services. The enslaveable communities are less favored in terms

---

[100] Department of Elementary Education and Literacy, Government of India, not dated.

[101] It is important to mention that the implementation of such affirmative action programs fall short of their targets, in some states in India. For example, the state government of Assam failed to fill almost 30,000 backlogged posts reserved for the ST, and the misuse of government funds allocated for SC/ST development projects. Additionally, the widespread government corruption led to misuse of funds designated to develop tribal areas (Chakma, 2007, pp. 27-28, pp. 107-108).

[102] The meso scale refers to communities, groups, networks, and local jurisdictions (Barrett and Swallow, 2006, p. 8). Mesoeconomics lies between the microeconomic (e.g., individual consumers, firms, and markets) and macroeconomic (the aggregate economy) theories (Walz-Chojnacki, 1999).

of location (usually at the periphery of urban regions, slums, shantytowns, and poor rural regions). They typically lack public physical infrastructures such as roads, electricity, water and sanitation systems; social infrastructures such as schools, health clinics, credit and banking services. They suffer from multiple formal-institution deficiencies, such as the absence of property-rights laws, lack of political power or representation, corrupt (or absence of) government agencies, e.g., police, courts, and other public services. These dismal conditions crowd out private investment by inflating the cost of market participation, such that the residents in these marginalized communities settle for low-return semi-subsistence production and low standards of living, which, in turn, reduce commercial and government incentives to intervene in these communities and regions. Therefore, there is a critical need for safety nets, above critical thresholds, to prevent the poor and vulnerable groups from falling back into chronic poverty. These safety nets insure sufficient consumption levels and reduce decumulation of assets owned by or distributed to the enslaveables, associated with giving authority over these resources and public services to the lowest possible scale, such as the enslaveable communities (Barrett and Swallow 2006, p. 11).

National intervention is the most suited to initiate, amend, and/or remove specific formal rules and statutory laws. With the aim of eradicating MDS practices through the enhancement and enforcement of existing anti-MDS laws, national interventions also can toughen the punishments against MDS perpetrators and their collaborators, and implement policies and programs to rescue the victims and reduce the enslaveables' vulnerability.[103] Government's intervention

---

[103] According to the Commission for Scheduled Caste/Scheduled Tribes, Delhi, the average number of registered (usually the more severe) cases of discrimination and atrocities decreased 1116 in 1997, from its peak of 4911 in 1997 (Thorat, 2002). This reduction, in part, can be attributed to the government's enactment of more anti-discrimination acts such as the Bonded Labour System (Abolition) Act of 1976, and the Scheduled Caste and Tribes (Prevention of Atrocities) Act of 1989, in addition to more effective enforcement of such acts. Furthermore, in

though collective bargaining and protective labor laws (such as minimum wage rates and affirmative action programs to protect the interest of minority groups) serves to empower the enslaveables and increase the cost of MDS industries.

In addition, the effective presence of government and non-government organizations can play a significant role in terms of increasing public awareness of MDS practices, by disseminating specific information on such practices and improving the effectiveness of government interventions. Such organizations can also act as viable interest groups and second sources for MDS victims and the enslaveables, to help rescue them and reduce their vulnerability.[104]

State and national governments should take advantage of the gradual shifting of the economy from the local level to the national and global levels, in terms of encouraging labor mobility, outside employment, and land reforms, etc.[105] Such policies tend to reduce caste value over time, as upper-caste members become more interested in cash and profit than service and prestige (Kolenda, 1966, p. 20). Studies show that increasing numbers of individuals who migrate to urban centers for employment return with stories of the changing and developing state of the world beyond the village (Rowe, 1966, p. 41). Studies also show that labor mobility and living within urban proximity are associated with less child labor, higher school attendance, overall improvement in child welfare, and higher wellbeing for the vulnerable population groups (Fafchamps and Wahba, 2006, p. 2). The supply and demand for labor in and around cities are likely to reduce child

---

1997, the Supreme Court of India ordered The National Human Right Commission (NHRC) in India to supervise states' implementation of bonded labor laws, which, in turn, began to pressure certain industries and states to implement and observe such laws (Human Rights Watch, 2003).

[104] India's National Human Rights Commission (NHRC) has proposed and lobbied for teaching human rights in schools' standard curricula. Some universities responded by offering courses on human rights (U.S. DOS, 2006a, Section 4).

[105] The abolition of Landlordism in India in 1950 has had significant effect on inter-caste economic relations, which had shaken the foundations of economic and social structure of the Indian village. The high caste ex-landlords are no longer the arbitrators in all matters of village life (Rowe 1966: 43)

labor in absolute terms, but increase the market share of work in child employment and income (ibid, p. 17).

Governmental policy of internal migration and labor mobility, especially to urban areas, reduces the vulnerability of the enslaveables, due to a higher wage income, in comparison to subsistence income, mostly in-kind, in rural areas. This policy is likely to increase parental income and induce them to keep their children in school. In addition, the higher demand for literate workers, accompanied by higher wages for urban workers, increases the direct benefit from education there. Fafchamps and Shilpi (2005) refer to the complementary hierarchies (such as hospitals, schools, public administration) that generate higher return to education. Consequently, the supply of schools is likely to be higher in urban areas, in part, in response to the higher demand for schooling there. Of course, the government may opt to provide these services – hospitals, schools, and public administration – in comprehensive rural development plans, in cases of rural regions inhabited mostly by the poor and vulnerable groups. In cases of regions inhabited by segregated groups in disputes, the government may opt to relocate the vulnerable groups to communities where they do not face discrimination.

1.2.3 International interventions and remedies

International interventions should be rooted in compliance with, and observance of, the United Nations' 1948 Universal Declaration of Human Rights, with special attention to the following articles, which are clearly against the many dimensions of MDS practices (The United Nations, 1948).

Article 1: All human beings are born free and equal in dignity and right.

Article 4: No one shall be held in slavery or servitude, and slavery and slave trade shall be prohibited in all their forms.

Article 5: No one shall be subjected to torture or to cruel, inhuman, or degrading treatment or punishment.

Article 8: All are equal before the law and are entitled without any discrimination to equal protection of the laws.

Article 23: The right to equal pay for equal work

Article 24: The right to rest, and leisure, including reasonable limitation of working hours and periodic holidays with pay

Article 25: The right to a standard of living adequate for the health and well-being of himself and of his family

Article 26: The right to education, such that education shall be free, at least in the elementary and fundamental stages, and elementary education shall be compulsory.

In addition, the following international conventions, declarations, and protocols specifically prohibit modern-day slavery and similar practices: Slavery Convention, 1927; Forced Labour Convention, 1932; Convention for the Suppression of the Traffic in Persons and of the Exploitation of the Prostitution of Others, 1949; Convention for the Suppression of the Traffic in Persons and of the Exploitation of the Prostitution of Others, 1951; Supplementary Convention on the Abolition of Slavery, the Slave Trade, and Institutions and Practices Similar to Slavery, 1956; Abolition of Forced Labour Convention, 1959; Forced Labour Convention, 1959; Convention on the Elimination of All Forms of Discrimination against Women (CEDAW), 1979; and, International Convention on the Elimination of All Forms of Racial Discrimination,1990.[106]

Such a universal standard is required to sustain and protect the human capability, especially of the vulnerable groups in each country or society. Governments of all nations should implement certain universal standards that satisfy "the bare minimum of what respect for human dignity requires" (Nussbaum, 2000, p. 5). Under this universal capability approach, each individual

---

[106] For a full list of the International Human Rights Instruments related to MDS practices, see the Office of the United Nations Office of the High Commissioner for Humans Rights (UNHCHR) http://www.unhchr.ch/html/intlinst.htm.

is treated as an end. This approach should be committed to cross-cultural norms of justice, equality, and rights, yet remain sensitive to local particularity, e.g., beliefs and preferences.

In addition, the human capability approach, pioneered by Amartya Sen and Martha Nussbaum, emphasizes that certain rights are required and cannot be surrendered, even with the promise of other substitutes or rewards. Nussbaum (2000) emphasizes that all capabilities are equally fundamental; for example, economic needs should not be met by denying liberty, and vice versa (p. 7).[107] The list of human functional capabilities covers, but is not limited to: life; bodily health; bodily integrity; senses, imagination and thought; emotions; practical reasoning; social affiliation; and, control over one's political and material environment.[108] Nussbaum (2000, pp. 49-52) has responded to the two major objections to universal values, such as the ones stated above. The first criticism opposes universal values in favor of the good of diversity in different countries/societies. Types of diversity that are compatible with human dignity and other basic values should be preserved, such as languages and arts. However, discriminating traditional practices that harm people, or targeted groups of people, (e.g., SC/ST in India, aboriginal tribes such as the *Dinka* in South Sudan, the

---

[107] For further analysis of the human capability approach and its relation to human rights and development, see Nussbaum (2000) and Sen (1999 and 2002).

[108] Other differentiated categories of human capabilities include *basic capabilities* (such as seeing, hearing); *internal capabilities*, which occur as part of the natural aging process, such as learning to speak a native language or sexual functioning, and other capabilities that develop with surrounding support, such as how to play with others, love, and the exercise of political choice. *Combined (or external) capabilities* combine the internal capabilities and external conditions that support the exercise of the function. The victims of MDS and similar practices are typically denied the combined capabilities. For example, the SC/ST in India, who are raised without freedom of speech, social affiliation, and religion, do not develop the same sense of political, social, and religious capabilities as the upper-caste population. This, in turn, heightens the vulnerability of SC/ST and exposes them to intense discrimination and MDS practices. For details on these lists/categories, see Nussbaum (2000, pp. 78-86). International interventions should seek the protection and provision of combined capabilities by promoting the external conditions that support the functioning of the internal capabilities, especially for the marginalized population groups, the enslaveables.

Black-Moors population in Mauritania, and women in many countries, especially in LDCs) are not worth preserving simply because they exist, or because they are inherited, generation after generation. The second criticism refers to the imposition of such universal values as a form of paternalism that should be opposed because it leaves little room for people's freedom and right to choose what suits them. However, tolerance, freedom, and other major liberties are themselves universal values, which require a universalist account, for their recognition and their protection against those who do not want other people to make choices for themselves. Universal values aim to protect vulnerable population groups from the discriminating paternalistic norms and traditions present in many countries and societies. Summarizing the above, Nussbaum notes, "More generally, any system of law is 'paternalistic,' keeping people from doing something that they want to do" (p. 54).

Effective international intervention should be accompanied by effective reward-punishment mechanisms, to support and reward governments that cooperate in eradicating MDS practices, while imposing effective economic and political sanctions against governments that fail to intervene in eradicating, or are apathetic to, such practices. Examples of such sanctions include economic and political restrictions. International intervention should accommodate the specifics and uniqueness of MDS practices in different countries and within each country. In addition, international and foreign countries' interventions should prosecute the citizens from these foreign countries who participate as customers or collaborators in MDS industries in LDCs, such as the child sex tourism trade and in the sex sector/industries overall, where MDS victims are forced to serve these customers. These countries should also prosecute MDS perpetrators who participate in trafficking MDS victims into their countries, and the collaborators who knowingly use MDS industries in LDCs to extract enslavement rent through the importation of low-cost MDS goods (e.g., hand-woven scarves, carpets, *beedi* cigarettes, glassware).[109]

International/foreign aid and assistance programs range from very broad aid, such as social and economic development and poverty-reduction assistance programs, to aid tied to specific designations, such as to develop very poor communities, reduce the vulnerability of, or empower, the enslaveable groups. Finally, there is very specific aid that targets the interests of MDS victims and the enslaveables.[110]

International NGOs (e.g., American Anti-Slavery Group, Anti–Slavery International, Coalition against Trafficking in Women, Free the Slave, Human Rights Watch, International Justice Mission) play very crucial roles in forming and modifying international interventions, since they have first-hand experience, and an effective presence in countries where human rights' violations and MDS practices are widespread. The visibility and effective presence of international NGOs in LDCs allows them to serve as international watchdogs, reporting these practices, and exposing local and national corrupt officials and practices. International NGOs provide critical information that helps foreign countries and international organizations to form proper policies and interventions regarding MDS practices. Furthermore, they are equipped to serve as local representatives

---

[109] The rate of prosecution against child sex tourism has increased in recent years. Currently, more than 32 countries mostly developed countries) have extraterritorial laws that allow the prosecution of their citizens who engage in child sex tourism in foreign countries (mostly in LDCs). In response, the World Tourism Organization (WTO) established a task force to combat child sex tourism. In 1999, international organizations such as the WTO, NGOs, and other travel companies signed a global Code of Conduct for the Protection of Children from Sexual Exploitation in Travel and Tourism. By 2005, 100 travel companies from 18 countries had signed this code (U.S. DOS, 2006b, Section I).

[110] The Indian government has participated in the ILO's International Program on the Elimination of Child Labor (IPEC) since 1992. Approximately 145,000 children have been removed from work, and received education and stipends though IPEC programs. In addition, since 1999, the South Asian Coalition of Child Servitude (SACCS) has freed more than 55,000 children from the work force (U.S. DOS, 2006a, Section 6).

of international organizations, in charge of implementing and managing international aid and assistance to the poor and enslaveables and prevent any transfer practices (that prevent foreign aid from reaching the poor and enslaveables). They seek specific aid and programs that fit the particular needs, based on the situation of the enslaveables, MDS practices, and the level of local governments' cooperation or corruption.

Limitations on international interventions include the lack of effective enforcement, potential conflict with particular/peculiar 'sacred' beliefs and cultural norms in LDCs, and misunderstanding of the particular causes and schemes of MDS practices in different countries. False paradigms, a lack of knowledge regarding specific MDS practices, the effective presence of interest groups, and public choice effects in LDCs (and, to some degree, in international and foreign aid organizations), can neutralize the effects of international intervention – if not by helping the MDS collaborators, then by transferring foreign aid away from the victims and the enslaveables.

2. Special Considerations for Effective International Interventions

The following numbered paragraphs discuss the special considerations necessary for effective international interventions against modern-day slavery:

1. Poor people, not poor countries, are the victims of poverty and poverty-linked practices such as modern-day slavery.

> Programs aimed at raising general or average well-being do not improve the situation of the least well-off, unless they go to work directly to improve the quality of those people's lives. Martha Nussbaum (2000, p. 56)

Rescuing and assisting victims should precede efforts and interventions to rescue and assist poor countries. The poor are people, not countries! There is a significant misconception regarding the difference between poor countries and the actual poor in these countries, due to widespread dualism,[111] skewed distribution of power, income and wealth, and institutional foundations leading to the marginalization of the enslaveables. LDC governments' programs, and foreign assistance programs in LDCs, should include specific clauses that address and provide for the basic needs of the poor and vulnerable, and aid in the development of poor communities, such as slums, shantytowns, and marginalized rural communities (Streeten 1981 and1998).

2. Foreign debt reduction or forgiveness (recall Britain's Jubilee 2000 Coalition for Debt Relief), and further foreign assistance should be utilized to help MDS victims and the enslaveables in LDCs. Programs similar to existing debt-for-environment swaps, or perhaps the better termed "debt-for- redemption swaps" or "debt-for-human dignity swaps," should be adopted by international and foreign lenders and donors, in order to level the playing field for MDS victims and the enslaveables. Under such swaps, foreign debt (or a portion of it) will be forgiven in exchange for the debtor LDC government's commitments and effective implementation of anti-MDS programs, in terms of eradicating MDS practices, reducing the enslaveables' vulnerability and empowering them, and developing poor and marginalized communities.

A major advantage of such swaps is the collective interest and involvement of LDC governments, foreign governments, and NGOs (local and international) in programs designated to help the poor and marginalized. It is especially advantageous in poverty-stricken regions such as ignored rural regions, slums, and shantytowns. Such programs reduce the vulnerability of the enslaveables and empower them by reducing their level of desperation, and providing viable second sources such as the presence of NGOs, and education,

---

[111] Dualism refers to the chronic coexistence of increasing divergences between the haves and have-nots, such as urban regions and rural regions, or modern sectors and traditional sectors, or the elite class and the marginalized population, especially in LDCs.

credit, and employment opportunities that accompany such swap programs. The characteristics of these various swaps should depend on the effectiveness of LDC governments' anti-MDS programs, the state of living of enslaveables and other poor in LDCs.

3. Who benefits from foreign aid to the poor in LDCs? "Foreign aid makes it possible for ... societies to transfer wealth from the poor [the general populace] to the rich [the rulers of third world countries and their hanger-ons]" (Osterfeld, 1994, p. 201). Dualism and widespread corruption explain, in part, the persistent coexistence of the very rich and the very poor in less developed countries. The more informed and powerful groups (including corrupt officials and MDS perpetrators) are often able to transfer most, if not all, foreign aid away from the enslaveables and marginalized communities (usually, the designated beneficiaries of foreign aid). Therefore, most, if not all, foreign aid bypasses the enslaveables and marginalized communities, since they are too uninformed and vulnerable to hold on to foreign aid that is more expensive and transferable (e.g., foreign brand-name clothes, electronics, and food supplies). Studies in rural India show that high transaction costs[112] associated with foreign aid to the poor and vulnerable can exceed the benefits from such programs. This is due to the prevalence of rent-seeking activities by corrupt officials and influential social groups that transfer foreign aid away from the poor and vulnerable: the intended beneficiaries of such aid. Corrupt local public officials can threaten to harm and retaliate against people who complain against them; they can even falsify reports and prosecute uncooperative citizens, especially the vulnerable (Gupta, 1995, pp. 381-383; Djankov, et al., 2006a).[113] Johnson and Blomqvist (1996), in their research on

---

[112] According to North (1990), transaction costs is, "the cost of measuring the valuable attribute of what is being exchanged and the cost of protecting rights and policing and enforcing agreements" (p. 27).

[113] Studies show that foreign aid is easily appropriated by corrupt government officials and elite groups in LDCs, since they are not subject to the same accountability measures as taxation, which is unpopular and less profitable. In addition, this finding explains the small effect

development aid and international rent seeking, underscore the above point: "...anecdotal evidence abound about aid ending up in the pockets of politicians, government officials and other members of the ruling elite... It is important for them to show evidence of a positive development despite the fact that part of the aid flow is diverted from its intended use" (pp. 5-6), to maintain the flow of foreign aid. Johnson and Blomqvist go on to explain the interest of rent-seekers in sustaining rent-seeking activities. "The problem for the rent seeker is to choose a rate of siphoning resources out of the system at a sustainable rate, considering the double risk of being thrown out of office and the donor discontinuing the aid flow" (p. 7). Influential social groups tend to have close and regular interaction to reduce the conflict of interest among them and to sustain their gain from foreign aid, at the expense of the socially marginalized and vulnerable groups in LDCs (Djankov, et al., 2006a, 2006b; Svensson, 2000).

Corrupt LDC governments and officials (at both the national and local levels) can sustain the flow of foreign aid through reports of false or exaggerated progress towards ending MDS practices in their countries or communities, assisting the enslaveables and MDS victims, and prosecuting MDS perpetrators and their collaborators.

This issue becomes more important and complex when the motives and intentions of the donors (e.g., government and non-government organizations, international organizations) are taken into consideration. Johnson and Blomqvist (1996) highlight three different motives of international donors: first, to satisfy political goals and commercial considerations; second, to satisfy a perceived moral obligation from historical wrongdoing and a desire to rectify past mistakes; and, third, to satisfy a moral imperative that stems from humanitarian reasons, i.e., conscience, Christian duty, etc. The first motive is likely to lead to a moral hazard

---

of foreign aid on economic development and economic growth, since foreign aid induces many rent seeking activities (Djankov, et al., 2006b).

problem by LDC governments (or the receiving agents in LDCs). The moral obligation usually ends when the aid is delivered to LDC governments, under the second motive. Both motives are subject to rent-seeking activities by LDC governments. The third motive is the one least-associated with rent seeking, when implemented properly (p. 10). It represents the sincere desire and aspiration of the donors to help the designated recipients of the aid directly, such as the poor and the vulnerable communities in LDCs, rather than helping LDC governments and government agencies, or trusting them to do so.

Local officials in many LDCs, especially in poor, rural regions, may represent a challenge to Western notions of the boundary between 'state' and 'society.' Corrupt officials collapse the distinction between their role as public servants and as private citizens (Gupta, 1995, p. 384). Therefore, international assistance programs should adopt the least-transferable forms of aid that are least likely to be confiscated or transferred away from the poor by MDS perpetrators and corrupt officials. These programs should also use more domestically-based aid, which is less costly and less transferable than foreign aid, and should be customized to fit the specific needs of the enslaveables and marginalized communities. Examples of least-transferable aid include the economical, domestically-produced aid, which has less exchangeable value, and community-based services that augment the enslaveables' human capital, such as education, training, employment, health clinics, banking, and credit services.

The above analysis applies also to national governments' interventions to help the enslaveables and MDS victims in local regions. Studies (e.g., Abraham and Platteau 2001; Galasso and Ravallion 2000; Ravallion and van de Walle 2001) show that when central resources are delegated to local organizations, the elite tend to appropriate whatever they need and leave the leftovers to the poor. The local elite, and public servants, can capture most of the benefits of national programs aimed at helping the poor and vulnerable groups in local regions. The local elite "sees the national intervention as an opportunity to enhance their position" (Ravallion and van de Walle, 2001, p. 2). They can capture the development resources by channeling such resources to themselves instead of channeling them to the poor (the targeted beneficiaries of such national development programs). In collectivist societies, everyone expects everyone else to respond according to the rules, which will lead to cooperative equilibrium. However, in segregated societies (elite versus marginalized, upper castes versus lower castes, or castes versus non-castes), there are significant barriers that prevent the vulnerable groups (marginalized, low castes, castes) from benefiting from such national development programs. For example, the enslaveables may not know of certain national programs, available to help them, or they may be living in dwellings segregated from the upper caste or other population groups (physical barriers).

Moreover, the enslaveables and MDS victims may be reluctant to disclose facts of malfeasance in which they have been the victims, in order to hide their weakness and their shame (psychological barriers). Information circulates well within, but not between, population groups. The elite groups are entitled to violate the rules or decisions, if their interests dictate them to do so (Abraham and Platteau, 2001, pp. 10-12). The marginalized group would not violate the rules because of their fear of external supernatural punishments or from guilt feelings, provoked by their belief that it is morally wrong to violate existing rules designed for the well-being of the community, or from their fear of punishment from community-oppressive practices. In such a case, the sphere of private and social life becomes so intertwined (ibid, p. 13). The elite population and MDS perpetrators may exploit their social capital to extract more rent from the enslaveables, and other vulnerable groups, who lack such capital. Proper intervention should furnish the enslaveables' social capital and redistribute status goods, to reduce the enslaveables' vulnerability and to empower them.

4. Development programs should be extended to construct and develop the basic physical infrastructure (e.g., roads, water and sanitation, and power and electricity), and social infrastructures (schools, health clinics, employment, banking and credit services) of poor areas that are inhabited by the very poor and marginalized. Such provisions provide sustainable community supports that are less transferable.

The World Bank's pro-poor development interventions, especially in rural regions (where most of the poor live) are examples of effective interventions that target the most vulnerable – women and the SC/ST (The World Bank 2001). These interventions include improvements in the physical infrastructure, by increasing access to sustainable drinking water and sanitation services, and improvements in social infrastructures, such as expanding health and education services to the poor, especially to girls and lower-caste children (The World Bank: India).

5. The effective role and presence of civil society organizations (CSOs) and non-government organizations (NGOs) is crucial, especially in light of widespread government corruption, rent-seeking, transferring schemes, and an absent or ineffective government presence. CSOs and NGOs should serve as a buffer between MDS perpetrators (and their collaborators) and the enslaveables and marginalized communities. They typically act on behalf of the enslaveables on multiple fronts: they face and respond to the advanced and sophisticated schemes of MDS perpetrators and their collaborators, create public awareness about MDS practices, stimulate reforms, and further government and non-government interventions (Gopakumar, 1998).

A recent report shows India's failure to demonstrate effective law enforcement, and persistence in inadequate local prosecutions. Increased trafficking across state lines makes investigation or prosecution, without central coordination, more difficult. However, according to the same report, "Indian NGOs are world leaders in their activities to fight trafficking" (U.S. DOS, 2004b).

Some NGOs, such as Bonded Labour Liberation Front/Movement, have worked to release MDS victims, especially bonded laborers.[114]

Cooperation among local, national, and international NGOs is vital to the success of anti-MDS interventions. Local NGOs, and the local presence of NGOs, have more direct information about specific MDS practices: who the perpetrators and the victims are, the specific nature of the enslaveables' vulnerability, the perpetrators' schemes, the presence (or lack) of local second sources, and the level of corruption at the local levels. Therefore, they have an edge regarding the governance of transactions (or contracts) leading to MDS practices, such that their presence provides immediate and direct support to the MDS victims and the enslaveables. They also play a role in fostering local initiatives and community-based programs that are crucial for the development of poor and marginalized regions (Madison, 1998). Local NGOs are also able to utilize information disseminated in the vernacular media about local corruption and abuses, and to report and intervene against such acts (Gupta, 1995, p. 387). This may explain the important role of local NGOs, especially NGOs that are equipped with the proper cultural and social capitals.

National NGOs are better-suited to deal with nationally-based MDS practices, such as the intra-national trafficking of MDS victims, forced prostitution, forced pornography, pedophilia rings, and forced labor in some exporting industries (such as manual and hand-woven rugs, scarves, *beedi* cigarettes). They are equipped to train government officials regarding MDS practices and the laws/acts against these practices,[115] and mobilize efforts to reform formal institutions, in terms of initiating new laws, repealing and

---

[114] *Dandhua Mukti Morcha* (The Bonded Labour Liberation Movement) in India, reports that it released over 172,000 bonded laborers, including 26,000 children.

[115] The training of government officials in Kanrantaka, India, by NGO Jeevika (Jeeta Vimukti Karnataka- a), led to a sharp increase in the number of identified bonded laborers (Human Rights Watch, 2003).

amending existing laws and legislation, and enforcing them effectively. National NGOs may serve as public interest groups (or citizen groups), serving the general public, and as special interest groups, serving the interest of the vulnerable groups (the enslaveables) and MDS victims, by influencing and lobbying for government policies to empower the vulnerable groups (e.g., poor communities' development programs). They may lobby to repeal existing laws and legal loopholes that protect MDS perpetrators and industries, press for policy changes to protect the interest of MDS victims and the enslaveables, and enforce the laws against MDS perpetrators and practices. Furthermore, NGOs can give MDS victims, and the enslaveables, more access to higher-level authorities and can persuade higher-level officials (e.g., at the state or national government levels) to offset corruption at the local levels (Gupta, 1995, p. 383).

NGOs can also mobilize their presence as information agencies, able to sway international donors and assistance organizations to put more pressure on LDC governments to eradicate MDS practices, help the enslaveables, and develop the marginalized communities.

International NGOs are more-suited to disseminating information regarding governmental policies and practices regarding human rights, influencing the role of foreign corporations in eradicating MDS practices in their transactions or operations in LDCs, and informing international donors and foreign aid programs against such practices in LDCs. Furthermore, international NGOs play a very important role in the pursuit to eradicate modern-day slavery and level the playing field for the enslaveables and marginalized communities in LDCs. Their freedom to express their opposition to such practices and their ability to publish their findings without fear of oppressive government rules in some LDCs, especially where modern-day slavery is widespread, is extremely valuable. International anti-MDS NGOs have better information regarding the international trafficking of MDS victims and the globalization of MDS practices. They become the voice of voiceless victims (and local NGOs) in LDCs. They play a crucial role, representing and influencing decisions made by foreign donors (including international organizations), and corporations (including multinational corporations) that operate in LDCs, rewarding the cooperating governments and corporations that have effective anti-MDS records, and penalizing those involved in MDS practices. In summary, NGOs should utilize their influences at the local, national, and international levels as specific kinds of power (Basu, 1986).

6. Foreign/international interventions, especially international NGOs operating in LDCs, should be perceptive to embedded 'sacred' beliefs and cultural norms in LDCs, especially those beliefs and norms that seem controversial. These embedded beliefs and cultural norms are deeply rooted in LDCs' cultures and may require decades or centuries to change or eradicate. Diligence and a focus on helping MDS victims and the enslaveables are key elements to successful international interventions, which can often be foiled by local resistance to the foreign/imported cultural norms that accompany foreign aid, and the presence of international NGOs. Also, MDS perpetrators and their collaborators, including corrupt government officials, may demonize the intention of foreign/international intervention (including international NGOs), by distributing propaganda against 'foreign' interventions, and inciting popular rejection of such intervention and presence. As a result, MDS perpetrators can perpetuate MDS practices, thereby avoiding costly confrontations with such international interventions.

International interventions should not equate the entirety of a culture with old or change-resistant elements. For example, India is the most diverse in the world. It has seventeen official languages, four predominantly institutionalized religions with their own legal systems, and huge regional differences, as well as differences between class and caste, rural and urban, matrilineal and patrilineal, secularism and religiosity, and between nationalism and mysticism (Nussbaum, 2000, pp. 46-47). This means that simplistic, one-size-fits-all, solutions will not likely work. Instead, difficult as it may be, foreign intervention should be customized to fit the specific causes, needs, modes, and forms of intervention, to ensure the effectiveness of each intervention.

Effective foreign/international interventions should also cooperate with national and local communities and NGOs to minimize potential conflict or rejection of foreign aid and the presence of foreign/international NGOs in LDCs. It is necessary for international intervention to gain the trust of LDC governments, and more importantly, the trust of the poor, enslaveables, and marginalized communities.

7. International interventions should have a clear agenda: serve the interests of the MDS victims and the enslaveables, prosecute MDS perpetrators, and eradicate MDS practices. Competing interests (or hidden agendas) may divert needed energy and resources, may be unwelcome, and are likely to be exploited by MDS perpetrators, to neutralize or reject such interventions. Effective intervention must be transparent. The presence of competing or hidden interests may end up harming, rather than helping, MDS victims and the enslaveables. International/foreign agencies and NGOs should take into consideration the external effect of their intervention in LDCs. Successful intervention will make further efforts more acceptable and less susceptible to false claims by MDS perpetrators and their collaborators, against the intention of such intervention, and vice versa.

8. Effective international intervention should avoid the use, or the imposition, of inappropriate modes or programs (false-paradigm effect) on LDCs. Effective interventions should respond to the specific needs, cultural contexts, and causes and forces behind MDS practices in different communities in LDCs. Additionally, international intervention should coordinate with national and local government agencies and NGOs in LDCs to ensure effective interventions against MDS practices.

International interest and intervention against MDS and other similar practices should take into consideration the cultural and traditional barriers, especially those manipulated by the elite and winners of such cultures and traditions (usually at the expense of other victims, e.g., marginalized and vulnerable groups). Interventions should be sensitive to national and local cultures – especially, interventions that are accompanied by foreign aid. Foreign intervention should utilize universal norms of human capabilities without calling them Western or Christian, for example. Domestic propaganda, initiated by the winners of discriminating norms and traditions (e.g., upper castes, MDS perpetrators, and corrupt public servants) against foreign intervention, usually aims to discredit the intention of foreign intervention. The only exception is when MDS perpetrators and their collaborators control or capture most of the foreign aid and are able to prevent the distributional effects of foreign aid programs that aim to assist the victims (e.g., minority, vulnerable and poor groups) of domestic discriminating traditions and norms. The accusations of westernization and cultural colonialism are usually used in totalitarian regimes/communities to pre-empt the foreign intervention from taking effects. Therefore, foreign intervention should emphasize and take advantage of the national and domestic social and cultural initiatives that already exist in LDCs, at least at the formal level (Nussbaum, 2000, pp. 36-37).

Smart foreign intervention should also utilize all internal initiatives that are still rooted in the culture (before being corrupted), using secularist and moderate views – without calling them secularist (since such a term is not acceptable in certain countries and communities). Also, international intervention should take into consideration the specific historical and legal backgrounds associated with complex phenomena such as modern-day slavery. However, neglecting the variety and complexity of traditions that lead to appalling phenomena such as modern-day slavery is wrong and offensive (ibid, pp. 40-41).

9. Rethink the rationale of eliminating child labor and worldwide bans on trading goods produced by child labor: such interventions may fall short of rescuing MDS victims.[116] Outright bans on trading goods produced by child labor is another example of false paradigms that are based on modern practices in developed countries, which neither fits LDCs nor helps the children and the poor there. Banning child labor without ensuring the prerequisites for successful bans that should serve the interest of these children and their families is likely to increase their vulnerability and exposure to worse forms of MDS practices. The ban on child labor, per se, will not benefit these children, if their families depend on their wages and they have no viable alternatives, such as free education. The lack of child care at home, due to the absence of schools or the inadequacy of educational services,[117] the lack of adult employment (or adult wages that are below the subsistence level[118]), the absence of parents, and the prevalence of dire poverty, must be considered as well. Studies also show that most children and adult workers in the export-oriented apparel industry are female; limiting the export or regulating the industry hurts women and their dependents disproportionately.[119] Rita Panicker, director of a rehabilitation center for child workers in New Delhi, summarized this dilemma: "What worries me is that it is very easy to ban things. What happens next is much more difficult" (Gentleman, 2006). Many NGOs are reluctant to take an equivocal stand against child labor in

---

[116] About 30,000 to 50,000 child and young workers were thrown out of textiles factories in Bangladesh between 1993 and 1994, due to the suppliers' fear of losing their business (The Economist, 1995b).

[117] In many poor regions in India, schools exist on paper only, with lack of reliable electricity, medical service, water, decent roads. Many local functionaries are corrupt and teachers do not report for work in many poor regions (Nussbaum, 2000, p. 28).

[118] Basu (1999) presents a model of the relation between child labor and adult wage rates. Child labor exists when the adult wage rate falls below a minimum level.

[119] ILO investigations show that the wage rate is significantly higher in some exporting sectors, with better safety records, than wage rates in alternative employment (Hasnat, 1995). In addition, most child laborers work for local companies/markets, and the masters are politically powerful (The Economist, 1996).

poor communities in LDCs, for the above reasons (Nussbaum, 2006, p. 29); they prefer to provide supplemental after-hour schooling for working children.

International interventions should not only consider the legal interests of multinational corporations or their branches in LDCs, but also the interest of the child laborers and their families. The spirit of such a ban on child labor is to protect the children's interest and provide them better opportunities, assuming the availability of such opportunities, such as school for children and employment for their parents, to compensate for the lost income from child labor. Appropriate measures to rescue MDS victims, prevent further MDS practices, and help the enslaveables and marginalized communities should be considered when making policy interventions in LDCs. Levi Straus, a maker of denim blue jeans, is a good example of proper intervention. It has provided schooling for child workers in its supplier's plant in Bangladesh (The Economist, 1995b). Eradicating MDS practices should take precedence over banning child labor, since MDS practices are 'the greater evil.' Banning child labor should be part of empowering the enslaveables, in terms of reducing the enslaveables' vulnerability, through adult employment and affordable education for children.

10. The critical role of external intervention against discriminating informal traditions and formal rules in LDCs (the practice of certain sensitive discriminating traditions and beliefs in some LDCs) may impose significant barriers on the victims of such practices, and on local NGOs, preventing them from opposing or resisting such practices. Their fear of further discrimination and persecution by the powerful and influential groups (the winners and beneficiaries of such discriminating practices) prevents them from voicing their opposition or complaining about the harm or discrimination inflicted on them from these practices. International/foreign organizations, including NGOs, are the most suited to exposing such unfair practices, and initiating interventions on behalf of the victims of such practices. First, they are not obliged (compared to national and

local organizations) to abide by these practices. Second, they can refer to universally accepted human rights laws and conventions and demand their implementation in all countries and communities. Third, they can mobilize economic programs, such as foreign/international aid and debt reductions for cooperating countries, stage boycotts and impose economic sanctions against countries that fail to oversee human rights laws and conventions at the national or local levels. Fourth, they seek to level the playing field by providing equal access to the enslaveables and marginalized communities, based on universally established conventions and rules against potential LDC governments' reactions or justification of such discriminating practices against the enslaveables or marginalized communities in their countries. Fifth, international/foreign organizations are more effective in defending and protecting the interests of resisting victims and local dissenters who reject discriminating informal norms and formal rules that are generally accepted in certain countries/societies. It is important to send a clear message to the victims, and dissenters too, that they will be protected and supported by international organizations, which, in turn, empower national and local organizations in LDCs to tackle discriminating 'tabooed' or 'sacred' traditions (and/or formal rules) against the enslaveables and marginalized communities.[120]

11. Government agencies and NGOs should initiate and/or support the building of social capital and the redistribution of status goods (or positional goods) in favor of the poor and vulnerable communities. They should work to augment the enslaveables' social networks, and improve their holding of status goods (at the expense of the elite, upper castes, and MDS perpetrators). These actions can reduce the enslaveables' transactions costs, associated with the search

---

[120] Nisha Sharma resisted her in-laws' demand for dowry payments (legally banned, under the Dowry Prohibition Act of 1961, yet widespread, especially in rural areas). Her refusal turned her into a national icon in India and led to copycat effects among other women in India, in addition to being covered by the international media, e.g., CNN (Haidar, 2003).

for employment or credit, and reduce their state of desperation, which, in turn, reduces their dependency on the offers of MDS perpetrators. In addition, the trust between intervening government/non-government agents and the enslaveables/MDS victims should be deepened and maintained, such that the enslaveables may respond properly to such interventions. MDS victims and the enslaveables are less likely to trust the intention of intervening agents; after all, they were forced to become MDS victims because of their initial trust in the MDS perpetrators and their scams of help. Effective interventions should deliver what is promised. As stated by Platteau (1994b), "trust corresponds to an attitude of initial predisposition to honesty subject to revision over time depending upon the degree of fulfillment of expectation" (p. 761). Also, according to Fafchamps (2004), trust refers to "the willingness of two or more individuals to enter into a negotiated agreement with each other, to incur obligations and to acquire rights that have only imperfect protection." (p. 155). The trust that failed when the enslaveables were victimized by MDS perpetrators (and corrupt government officials and public servants) must be restored. This can be accomplished by offsetting interventions by government and non-government organizations at all levels (local, national, and international) to rescue MDS victims, reduce the vulnerability of the enslaveables and empower them, and prosecute MDS perpetrators. Trust can be thought of as a form of social capital that accumulates through good actions and agents (e.g., NGOs) and dissipates through bad actions and agents, such as MDS perpetrators and their collaborators, and ineffective/apathetic intervening organizations (Fafchamps, 2004, p. 36). The good reputation of NGOs serves as a form of social collateral that reduces the vulnerability of the enslaveables, empowers them, and develops vulnerable communities, while also increasing the cost of MDS practices, which, in turn, reduces the enslavement rent. Therefore, the effective presence of NGOs and their commitments in poor and vulnerable communities in LDCs play a vital role against MDS practices.

12. Internal migration, relocation, and labor mobility should be considered and utilized as effective tools to reduce the vulnerability of the enslaveables living in collectivist communities, where they are forced to abide by rules and norms that discriminate against them.[121] The enslaveables and others (e.g., members of certain minority communities) are generally looked upon with suspicion and considered potential enemies, in many collectivist communities. In contrast, the elite (including upper castes, public servants and MDS perpetrators) share a strong feeling of collective identity, which distinguishes them from the poor and enslaveables, and use the discriminating norms and rules to benefit themselves – at the expense of the poor and enslaveables. Migration into less collectivist communities, such as urban centers, and new communities that free the enslaveables from their vulnerability, will take time. Studies show that children in wards where most adults engage in subsistence agriculture are less likely to undertake market work and more likely to engage in subsistence work and housework. Having farming parents is shown to have a net effect on child labor (Fafchmaps and Wahba, 2006, p. 29). This phenomenon follows a path of dependence, where these children are trapped in poverty and vicious cycles of vulnerability. The situation is more favorable for children with less work and more education, near urban centers.

13. Gender-based development programs are extremely important. Studies from Southern India show the significant effect of women's employment (especially away from their traditional communities), and, consequently, the

---

[121] Abraham and Platteau (2001), Luke and Munshi (2004), and (Fafchamps and Wahba (2006) are examples of many studies that recommend internal migration/mobility as an effective solution in collectivist societies, e.g., the SC/ST in many communities in India, especially rural communities.

increase in the share of their income and bargaining power within the household, especially among the low castes and the SC/ST. Their employment also has the propensity to increase the educational attainment of their children – especially their daughters (thus narrowing the gender gap in school in these groups) – as well as the propensity to distance themselves from their traditional economy and weaken their ties to their home community. These women emerged as independent agents of renewal. Therefore, national and international interventions, including NGOs, should empower the marginalized SC/ST and low-caste women as an essential ingredient in all interventions that seek to eradicate MDS practices, reduce the vulnerability of the enslaveables, and empower them. These women are less likely to return to poverty, and the discriminating cultural norms and traditions of abuse that accompanies it, in their inferior home communities. Instead, they prefer to move to larger communities or cities that are associated with relative anonymity. Longer schooling attainment among the low castes and SC/ST tends to change their behavior regarding inherited norms, such that it lowers their tendency to marry a relative or to move back to an ancestral location. Studies also show that children's school attainment increases with the distance from their original community locations (Luke and Munshi, 2004).

14. International interventions should also aim to enhance the capabilities of the enslaveables to function, since the enslaveables' existing/current functioning is limited to what the enslaveables (and MDS victims) may need to survive or aspire as victims – not as free people. The preferences and aspirations of MDS victims and the enslaveables are curtailed, given their past history and current state, and the hostile surrounding, social, political, and cultural environments that marginalize them and constrain their capabilities. International agencies should act on behalf of the enslaveables and MDS victims to promote their capabilities and functioning. However, responding solely to the needs of the

enslaveables (given their state of enslaveability) may have a transitory effect only. The enslaveables needs/aspirations are constrained or corrupted by their dire state and their lack of faith in the surrounding environments that have failed them and reduced them to enslaveable status, and even MDS victims.

Agents of international organizations should take into consideration that the choices and aspirations of marginalized groups are distorted due to unfavorable background conditions (Nussbaum, 2000, p. 114). Responses to distorted desires and choices are likely to be transitory, with no long-term effects. Without reversing the root causes of such distortions, international interventions can be manipulated to serve the interests of the elite population groups and perpetuate discriminating practices that are embedded in these communities' traditions and norms, such as MDS practices. The enslaveables and MDS victims may sign away their capabilities due to their vulnerability, dire poverty, and immediate need for help. Yet, such consents must not be used in defense or justification for any discriminating practices against them, including MDS practices.

15. International intervention (by foreign governments, international organizations, or international NGOs) should always assume and propose a dominant role for LDC governments, in their interventions against MDS practices in LDCs, to help the enslaveables, and in their plans to reduce the vulnerability of the enslaveables and to empower them. Such coordinated efforts provide a suitable and sustainable environment to embrace and implement the goals of international interventions. International interventions should also build on domestic and regional accomplishments and promising programs, taking advantage of the national and domestic cooperation and support for such ongoing programs.[122]

---

[122] See Nussbaum (2000) for examples of successful programs, such as those in the State of Kerala, India, and to apply them to other less successful or more resisting states, such as the States of Bihar and Andhra Pradesh, India (p. 103).

Chapter 5

Foundations for Effective Christian Interventions and Remedies: A Biblical Perspective

The Christian response to modern-day slavery should be a manifestation of God's 'Redemption' for all victims of such a cruel and appalling manifestation of "The Fall." Christian perspectives should reflect the new redeemed identity and calling, as God's faithful servants and active agents of renewal, to transform the fallen practices into God's intended Kingdom. Christians are called to bring justice to this fallen world, to be the voice of the voiceless, to defend the defenseless, to rescue the victims, to protect and help the vulnerable, and to intervene wisely against the oppressors and rebuke them – whenever and wherever such fallen practices of oppression occur.[123] The following non-exhaustive discussion list emphasizes the importance of Christian concerns and interventions, and guide Christian interventions that take into consideration the many sides and nature of intricate problems such as modern–day slavery.

1. Christians are called to redeem the victims of fallen practices

The scroll of the prophet Isaiah was handed to him. Unrolling it, he found the place where it is written: "The Spirit of the Lord is on me, because he has anointed me to preach good news to the poor. He has sent me to proclaim freedom for the prisoners and recovery of sight for the blind, to release the oppressed, to proclaim the year of the Lord's favor." (Luke 4: 17-19)

Redeeming victims of "The Fall" is integral to Christian faith and the role of Christians as active agents of renewal, transforming fallen practices into God's

---

[123] The term 'Christians' may refer to Christian individuals, communities, and/or organizations, according to the context. 'Christian organizations' may refer to Christian churches, CSOs, NGOs, charities, and so forth.

intended Kingdom. Redeeming the poor, freeing the prisoners, and releasing the oppressed were integral to Jesus' ministry. These verses reflect God's utmost care and plan to rescue the victims (the prisoners and oppressed), reduce the vulnerability of poor, and empower them.

Jesus' intervention to rescue the victims and help the vulnerable is a reflection of God's own interest in redeeming, transforming, interventions. In the case of modern-day slavery, Christians should follow Jesus' lead through effective intervention to rescue MDS victims, reduce the vulnerability of the enslaveables, and develop marginalized communities.

Christians are called to intervene on behave of the victims of fallen practices, spreading and sharing the good news of salvation and redemption to all victims, by helping the poor, rescuing the victims, seeing for the blind, speaking for the voiceless, and defending the defenseless.

2. Strong convictions and an effective presence in harsh environments

I am the good shepherd. The good shepherd lays down his life for the sheep. The hired hand is not the shepherd who owns the sheep. So when he sees the wolf coming, he abandons the sheep and runs away. Then the wolf attacks the flock and scatters it. The man runs away because he is a hired hand and cares nothing for the sheep. (John 10: 11-13)

Finally, be strong in the Lord and in his mighty power. Put on the full armor of God so that you can take your stand against the devil's schemes. (Ephesians 6: 10-11)

We are hard pressed on every side, but not crushed; perplexed, but not in despair; persecuted, but not abandoned; struck down, but not destroyed. We always carry around in our body the death of Jesus, so that the life of Jesus may also be revealed in our body. (2 Corinthians 2: 8-10)

These verses shed light on attempts that failed to rescue MDS victims and help the enslaveables. These attempts failed due to a lack of genuine conviction in intervening and rescuing MDS victims, and the presence of competing interests, especially if they are less stressful than modern-day slavery, and/or because of the significant risk associated with effective intervention against cruel and more-organized MDS perpetrators.

Christians are called to be good shepherds. 'Good' refers to how faithful and steadfast Christians should be in reaching out, and their yearning to rescue and serve the victimized and unprotected groups, whose ability to defend themselves has been diminished significantly as a result of fallen and oppressive societal norms, beliefs, rules, and practices. Individuals and organizations with a strong calling to serve God, by rescuing the victims and helping the vulnerable in harsh and hostile environments, will be able to tolerate those harsh and risky environments by trusting in God and living in faith. Transforming such fallen practices and building civil societies with such a deep sense of purpose should be among the prized tasks of Christian interventions, including Christian NGOs that are motivated to stay and focus on the interests of MDS victims and the enslaveables (Hoksbergen, 1999 and 2005). The effective presence of Christian organizations is crucial; especially in the dreadful environments the enslaveables inhabit, such as shantytowns, slums, and marginalized rural communities. The lack of a basic infrastructure makes it difficult for government officials or NGO agents to remain in these communities to protect (or oversee) their tasks of rescuing MDS victims or helping the enslaveables.

Christian organizations and NGOs, motivated by their calling to serve God and their dedication to rescue MDS victims and help the enslaveables, are more likely to put up with the harsh and hostile MDS environments, pursue justice, and save MDS victims and empower the enslaveables (Zachariah 7: 9-10). On the contrary, appointed (or hired) self-interest officials and organizations are less likely to tolerate the deplorable living environment of MDS victims and the enslaveables, as well as the hostility and risk associated with challenging MDS perpetrators (and their collaborators) and prosecuting them. Hence, interventions against MDS practices can be a very unpleasant experience for the appointed agents and officials who do not have a keen calling to serve, or are apathetic to the interests of MDS victims and the enslaveables (Haugen, 1999, p. 105). Saving

MDS victims and the enslaveables from their dire poverty and vulnerability is integral to God's engagement and concern for the everyday existence of creation. Salvation – in the Biblical sense – is both earthly and spiritual, and redemption takes on flesh-and-blood relevance on earth and in heaven (Brown, 2004, pp. 164-165). The continuing presence of Christian organizations in such poor and hostile environments is vital, due to the slow nature of change in inherited discriminating norms and practices, and due to the resistance of the winners of such discriminating norms (such as the upper castes, and MDS perpetrators and their collaborators) to interventions that seek to eradicate MDS practices, rehabilitate MDS victims, and empower the enslaveables (Jeremiah 21: 12).

3. Defending the rights of the victims and the vulnerable, and speaking up for them

> Speak up for those who cannot speak for themselves, for the rights of all who are destitute. Speak up and judge fairly; defend the rights of the poor and needy. (Proverbs 31: 8-9)

Christians are called to act and speak on behalf of victims: to rescue and help them, and develop their communities. Typically, MDS practices bring about cruel punishments to victims (and their families) who complain, escape, or attempt to escape. Many victims are disappointed when they plead for help and intervention. Immense fear and despair gradually silence the voices of the victims and the destitute. The silence of these victims should not be interpreted as the absence of abuse and oppression, or that some interventions have already occurred. In this fallen world, the victims are silenced because such silence serves the interest of their perpetrators who gain, not only at the expense of enslaving these victims, but also at the expense of their silence, which prevents any intervention against such abuse and oppression. As a result, others must speak up for these voiceless victims.

These verses call on Christians to identify the voiceless victims, since the voiceless are too weary, ignorant, and may be reluctant to identify themselves as victims. In a fallen world, only people who can voice their complaints can be heard and protected. Such ability to speak up is not accessible to all; the marginalized, disconnected, and outcast are likely to be deprived of the ability to speak for themselves as long as such deprivation serves the interests of their perpetrators. Consequently, effective interventions should reach out to locate, and be aware of these 'voiceless' victims in order to speak for them and intervene on their behalf. The Biblical call to speak up for the voiceless highlights the significance of effective presence in communities where oppressive practices such as modern-day slavery exist. Consequently, effective interventions should be accompanied by an actual presence in the marginalized communities (e.g., slums, shantytowns, and marginalized rural communities). Such interventions and presence increase the perpetrators' costs and risks, give a sense of hope to MDS victims and the enslaveables and increase their trust in redemptive interventions. These interventions reduce the enslaveables' vulnerability and desperation, mobilize further interventions (local, national and international) on behalf of the victims, and develop destitute communities – until they become able to speak for themselves and defend their own interests.

Nevertheless, the task of reaching out to, and speaking for, the voiceless can be tricky and delicate, since the voiceless victims are voiceless by design: first, to perpetuate the perpetrators' oppressive practices (and therefore perpetuate the oppressors' gains); second, to avoid raising any warning signals regarding the existence of such illegal, appalling, and oppressive practices (which may entice interventions); and, third, because of the victims' immense fear, mistrust, and weariness. Active reaching out to the voiceless victims should be at the heart of a Christian perspective and interventions on behalf of the voiceless.

4. The opposite positions of the righteous and the wicked

The righteous care about justice for the poor, but the wicked have no such concern. (Proverbs 29: 7)

Christians are called to step in and care about justice for the poor. The lack of concern about justice for the poor ranges from direct participation in oppressing the poor (e.g., enslaving MDS victims) and marginalizing the enslaveable communities, to passive positions and apathy. Such passive or apathetic attitudes implicitly endorse unjust practices, such as modern-day slavery, and heighten MDS victims' and the enslaveables' alienation. Such apathy regarding MDS practices also alienates us from MDS victims and the enslaveables. This alienation tends to heighten in the cases of oppressive practices such as modern-day slavery, which enslave "foreign" victims in "foreign" countries or communities.

God's special care and call for us to seek justice for the poor reflects to some extent our "fallen" alienation from the poor, who were victimized by sophisticated schemes based on greed and a lack of concern about human suffering and alienation. The poor were alienated by the acts of others: those who aim to gain at their expense and suffering. Yet, many alienate themselves further from these victims, either through apathy or passive intervention. Thus, effective participation in providing justice for the poor must be integral to our care about justice for the poor.

Christians should demonstrate their care for the causes of the poor and vulnerable by acting as effective second sources (to provide rehabilitation to rescued victims, information, education, legal support, employment, financial support and loans, etc., for the enslaveables and marginalized communities). If permitted, Christian organizations should intervene directly, or in partnership with other interest groups and second sources (Christian and non-Christian organizations, including NGOs and CSOs) that care about the well-being of the poor and have an effective record of helping the victims, reducing their vulnerability, and developing their communities (Marshall, 2005, pp. 246-48).

Christian caring about justice for the poor should be implemented in a way that ends with *providing* justice for the poor. Such care should be approached carefully and thoroughly, based on an understanding of the causes and schemes of discrimination, and oppressive practices such as modern-day slavery. It should also take into consideration the multiple layers and hierarchical structures of such oppressive practices, and their penetration into government agencies, such as corrupt police, judges, and other public servants, in additions to foreign collaborators (Haugen, 1999, p. 128). In addition, it should encompass effective intervention to transform the fallen institutional foundations of modern-day slavery, including the incomplete and imperfect governance of transactions, discriminating or ineffective formal rules, and the unfair and discriminating informal norms, traditions, and beliefs that are deeply embedded in societies.

Lastly, intervening Christian organizations should always be vigilant; otherwise, competing interests may sway them away from such a redemptive calling, such that they may be tricked to serve the interests of oppressors, such as MDS perpetrators, at the expense of the oppressed MDS victims and the enslaveables.

5. The crucial role of information and wisdom in offsetting the perpetrators' schemes

For wisdom will enter your heart, and knowledge will be pleasant to your soul. Discretion will protect you, and understanding will guard you. Wisdom will save you from the ways of wicked men, from men whose words are perverse. (Proverbs 2: 10-12)

Effective interventions should be based on discrete and detailed knowledge and understanding of modern-day slavery. Discerning and wise interventions, based on such information, are crucial to counterbalance the sophisticated schemes used by MDS perpetrators and their collaborators.

Christian organizations should take proper precautions and considerations to make their interventions effective. Transparent intentions are crucial for effective intervention to help the victims and enslaveables, and to develop the poor and marginalized communities in LDCs. Such transparent intentions, especially if supported by credible records, will pre-empt any claims by MDS perpetrators and their collaborators to discredit foreign or Christian interventions, especially in some non-Christian countries and communities.[124] Christian intervention against MDS practices in foreign countries must be approached with a high degree of discernment and shrewdness to avoid clashes with 'sacred' traditions and beliefs in LDCs, especially in the poor and marginalized communities there. Such interventions should focus on the goal – rescuing MDS victims, helping the enslaveables, and developing poor and marginalized communities in LDCs. Effective Christian interventions can take one or more of the following forms: the actual presence of Christian organizations in LDCs (e.g., churches and Christian NGOs); partnership between Christian organizations and other interested organizations, religious and secular, at all levels – international, national, and local – to benefit from their areas of specialization and success in LDCs; and, direct cooperation between Christian organizations and national and local LDC governments in their anti-MDS programs.

Proper intervention against MDS practices should also counterbalance the perpetrators' information advantage. Effective interventions, based on proper information and knowledge leading to wise anti-MDS interventions and strategies, should narrow the information gap between the perpetrators and the enslaveables and lower the perpetrators' information rent. This, in turn, will lower the enslavement rent and make MDS practices less lucrative or less practical for MDS perpetrators and their collaborators. Furthermore, the effective presence of Christian NGOs in LDCs – and the fostering of equal partnerships with local NGOs, especially in marginalized communities in LDCs – is extremely important

---

[124] The major claims against foreign/Christian interventions are, first, foreign intervention may contest widespread sacred traditions and beliefs in LDCs. Second, foreign interventions intend to serve foreign interests rather than the interests of the poor in LDCs. Third, the primary intention of Christian intervention is to proselytize and spread Christianity in LDCs. Interestingly, about 2000 years ago, the elite and rulers of the existing social order considered Jesus Christ, regardless of his nonviolence, a bandit. He was also executed as a bandit, by crucifixion (Brown, 2004, pp. 132-133).

in order to gain direct access to particular information that defines the most effective levels and forms of intervention, and the delivery of aid and assistance (Hoksbergen, 2005). It also enables Christian NGOs to counteract the schemes by MDS perpetrators and corrupt officials, who transfer such aid away from the targeted enslaveables and marginalized communities.

Christian interventions should also take into consideration the role of fallen spirituality or 'inner mechanism' in informal institutions, which corrupt and distort the formal institutions and the governance structure of transactions, and lead to the prevalence of appalling phenomena such as MDS. Saint Paul cited the role of fallen *powers, authorities, dominions,* and *principalities* (Romans 8: 38-39; 1 Corinthians 15: 24-26; Ephesians 1: 20-22, 2: 1-2, 3: 10 and 6: 12; Colossians 2: 14-15), and their manifestation in earthly institutions and human actions, in visible and invisible elements, which have penetrated and corrupted all spheres of human life (Brown, 2004, Chapter 6). These earthly institutions were part of God's good creation, but which have now acted in disobedience and opposition to God. Over time, such institutions gain power and have greater influence on humans, and become more autonomous from human control, with people's actions following complacently along these institutions' paths. However, all these powers and authorities have been exposed, disarmed, and "dethroned," by God's redemptive act and triumph over them, on the Cross (Colossians 2: 14-16). Christians are called to participate in redeeming this world, which includes redeeming fallen earthly institutions, renewing such institutions, and transforming them into God's intended Creation.

Effective intervention on behalf of the victims must discern the proper methods of intervention, forms of assistance, methods of delivery, and effectiveness of delivery to, and use by, the designated beneficiaries: MDS victims and the enslaveables. First, Christian organizations should identify the causes of poverty and the vulnerability of the enslaveables. Second, they should distribute their aid discerningly, to avoid transferring the aid away from the designated beneficiaries – MDS victims, the enslaveables and, marginalized communities – to MDS perpetrators, their collaborators, or other corrupt officials. Third, there should be an effective presence of Christian organizations, or their partners, in the marginalized communities. This presence will ensure that the poor receive help, prevent the transfer of aid, and act as an interest group (to press for more government interventions, in terms of security, access to legal services, and prosecution of MDS perpetrators). It will also provide effective second sources (by communicating the specific needs of the enslaveables and marginalized communities to their home organizations and other organizations). Fourth, Christian organizations should use the least-transferable forms of aid, such as education and adult vocational training, which benefits the poor and vulnerable. As stated by a poor Indian villager, "People think that education is the best form of investment. If your wealth is in land and money, you may have to share it with others. But your education can never be taken away from you" (Luschinsky, 1966, p. 68). Fifth, Christian organizations should use locally-produced goods, rather than relatively expensive and fancy foreign goods (such as brand name goods that induce transfer practices – particularly in the marginalized communities), which satisfy the basic needs of the enslaveables, yet are less likely to be transferred away from the designated beneficiaries. Sixth, Christian organizations should provide basic information and services, such as legal support services and health care centers, that empower the enslaveables, reduce their vulnerability, and narrow the information gap between MDS perpetrators and the enslaveables. This, in turn, can reduce the enslavement rent, and impose more pressure on the perpetrators and their collaborators to abandon MDS practices. Foreign policy-makers and citizens should be oriented to the situation in LDCs, especially the marginalized and poor communities in LDCs, before designing and implementing their intervention plans, to ensure effective and redemptive interventions that fit the needs of such communities (Nussbaum, 2000, p. 24).

6. Active participation

Learn to do right! Seek justice, encourage the oppressed.[a] Defend the cause of the fatherless, plead the case of the widow. [a] Or/ rebuke the oppressor. (Isaiah 1: 17).

Seeking justice, encouraging the oppressed (or rebuking the oppressors), defending the cause of the fatherless, and pleading the case of the widow, are God's clear command to Christians, to intervene as active agents of renewal on behalf of the actual victims and the vulnerable, and against the oppressors.

Christians are called upon to do right, to seek justice for the oppressed and persecuted, and to interfere on their behalf, because of their lack of access to legal help and other viable second sources, because of their inability to raise the required funds to seek justice, and because of their fear of the consequences and backlash against MDS victims and the enslaveables who seek help or speak up against MDS practices. Effective Christian interventions can provide viable second sources for the victims, and interest groups, to defend the interests and rights of the fatherless and widows; and, the most vulnerable to victimization – the enslaveables.

Effective rebuke of the oppressors should include intervening in MDS practices, exposing the collaborators, pressing for effective police presence and judicial procedures against the perpetrators, and prosecuting the perpetrators accordingly, to increase the costs and risks of MDS practices until such practices are abandoned.

7. Two-sided intervention: pro-victims and against perpetrators

I am sending you out like sheep among wolves. Therefore be as shrewd as snakes and as innocent as doves. (Matthew 10: 16)

The above verse sends a clear message for Christian active participation and involvement in transforming fallen practices and for intervening on behalf of the victims of such practices. God is sending us out into the world, to be active and filled with the spirit of love and care for the poor, the vulnerable, and the victims of fallen practices everywhere, including foreign countries and communities.

Christian intervention should take place on both sides of MDS practices, to rescue the victims, help the enslaveables, and develop marginalized communities. It should also push for effective law enforcement against the perpetrators and their collaborators. In the process, such redemptive and transforming interventions should take into consideration the harsh environment and high degrees of risk associated with oppressive practices such as modern-day slavery, especially in foreign countries or communities.

Christian organizations should be aware of the schemes and tactics of the perpetrators and their collaborators to neutralize, discredit, or even prevent Christian organizations' interventions, especially in foreign countries. Meanwhile, they should gain the trust of the victims, as viable support and interest groups against MDS practices, through effective presence and a legitimate pro-victims record. Adequate knowledge about the intentions and preferences of the Christian organizations reinforces the trust between the enslaveables and intervening Christian organizations, especially those that are in direct contact with the enslaveable communities. The effective presence of NGOs in poor and enslaveable communities is crucial in helping these communities, due to the difficulties they face in making contact outside their communities, their lack of social capital, and their distrust of corrupt public servants.

Ethical behaviors in non-business-related activities should be used to infer the Christian organizations' faith, and capacity to live up to their moral code (Fafchamps, 2004, p. 157).

Genuine interventions to redeem MDS victims and help the enslaveables are likely to face significant risk and harsh environments while challenging MDS perpetrators and their collaborators, who seek to sustain their gains from MDS practices. Christian organizations should take into consideration the perpetrators' vicious responses and condemnation. Staying focused, they should discern the most effective paths of intervention to offset the perpetrators' sophisticated schemes and their social and political influence (their collaboration with corrupt government officials).[125]

MDS perpetrators and their collaborators usually stand ready to face interventions by Christian organizations, to neutralize their presence, intimidate them, and make false claims to discredit the intention of such organizations, especially international and foreign organizations. Studies show that in certain societies when transactions take place with strangers (from different religions, languages, etc.), exchange is often equated to stealing or cheating. Cheating a foreigner (or a member from a different group) may even bring social prestige to the individual (Platteau, 1994a, p. 552). This is why Christian organizations should be cautious in their interventions. They must counterbalance the perpetrators and collaborators' schemes to discredit them, to neutralize their interventions, and even cheat them – all for the purpose of transferring foreign aid from the targeted MDS victims and the enslaveables to MDS perpetrators and their collaborators.

It is also feasible that some LDCs' governments, especially in non-Christian countries (or non-Christian communities), may reject intervention by "Christian" organizations. Yet, Christian organizations should not give in to such barriers (political, social, or cultural). They can still intervene indirectly, in alliance and partnership with other (international, national or local) organizations that have a stake in rescuing MDS victims, helping the enslaveables, and developing poor and marginalized communities, in these countries. The main message here is for Christian organizations to focus on their goal: to care for the

---

[125] Some Christian organizations report police harassment, such as surveying the number of Christians working in these organizations, punishing the SC/ST who convert to Christianity by revoking their affirmative action rights and benefits, and creating a rift among religious communities (Overdorf, 2003). The All-India Catholic Union (AICU), and other Christian organizations, expressed their concerns over violence against Christians in several states in India (U.S. DOS, 2005a, Section 2c).

well-being of the poor everywhere, and to affirm the unwavering Christian call to help them and intervene on their behalf, especially the victims and the most vulnerable.

God's call, in the above verse, refers to active participation and interventions on behalf of the victims of fallen practices. God is sending forth his active agents of renewal to save the victims of fallen and appalling practices that take place in other communities. Such interventions, on behalf of the victims, challenge the oppressors and perpetrators, who profit at the expense of these victims by using sophisticated schemes that are too complicated for the victims, who were stripped of all support in the process of being enslaved. Therefore, effective Christian interventions should be shrewd, in terms of gathering specific information, forming partnerships and alliances, proper timing and methods, and preparation for counterbalancing strategies by the perpetrators and their collaborators.

Wise intervention is very crucial when interventions take place in other (foreign) countries and communities, due to the presence of "undetectable" sacred traditions and taboos, which may be ignored or unknown by foreigners/outsiders (and which can be used both to enslave/abuse the victims, and against foreign interventions). Additionally, foreign interventions should be aware of the political, economic, and social influence of the perpetrators and their collaborators, such as corrupt politicians and public servants. Shrewd intervention should take into consideration the causes and forces behind MDS practices, as well as interventions against MDS practices by other groups, such as international organizations, foreign governments, other Christian and non-Christian organizations, and national and local governments and organizations in LDCs, to enhance the effectiveness of their interventions, and complement them. Such coordinated interventions among faith and development organizations underscore the synergy needed to eradicate MDS and similar practices in LDCs, save the victims, empower the enslaveables, and develop poor and vulnerable communities (Marshall, 2005, pp. 246-248).

8. Effective and redemptive interventions: the Good Samaritan

In reply Jesus said: "A man was going down from Jerusalem to Jericho, when he fell into the hands of robbers. They stripped him of his clothes, beat him and went away, leaving him half dead. A priest happened to be going down the same road, and when he saw the man, he passed by on the other side. So too, a Levite, when he came to the place and saw him, passed by on the other side. But a Samaritan, as he traveled, came where the man was; and when he saw him, he took pity on him. He went to him and bandaged his wounds, pouring on oil and wine. Then he put the man on his own donkey, took him to an inn and took care of him. The next day he took out two silver coins and gave them to the innkeeper. 'Look after him,' he said, 'and when I return, I will reimburse you for any extra expense you may have.' "Which of these three do you think was a neighbor to the man who fell into the hands of robbers?" The expert in the law replied, "The one who had mercy on him." Jesus told him, "Go and do likewise." (Luke 10: 30–37)

The 'Good Samaritan' is a model of redemptive interventions. Contrary to the apathy shown by the passing priest and the Levite toward the bleeding and half-dead victim, the Samaritan, a stranger, did not follow such a fallen pattern. Instead, his response began in his heart. He took pity on the victim, and that led him to intervene immediately, rescuing the victim, bandaging and pouring oil and wine on his wounds. He continued his care for the victim by taking him to an inn and paying for his expenses, thus reducing the victim's vulnerability. He remained present to ensure the well-being of the victim, visiting the recovering victim the next day and promising to continue to provide for the victim's care during his recovery. Christians, including Christian organizations, are called to act likewise toward MDS victims and enslaveables.

The Biblical definition of neighbor encompasses neighborly acts that reflect love and care for others. This is accompanied by a willingness to intervene directly, or on their behalf, especially when it matters most (i.e., the victimization of others, regardless of family ties, or other socially fallen ties, such as tribal, racial, ethnic, or religious ties or affiliations). Biblically, the concept of neighbor and neighborhood reflects the notion that all people belong to each other, and that redemptive acts by strangers (e.g., the Good Samaritan) make them true neighbors to the victims (in our growing globalized village). This is in contrast to the apathy revealed by the culturally fallen definition of neighbors.[126]

The relevance of the Good Samaritan story is that Christians should act neighborly toward foreign/alien victims of MDS practices that take place in foreign/alien countries. These victims are our neighbors in the sense of our love for them, and our willingness to intervene to save, and care for, them. Apathy and lack of intervention on behalf of foreign victims or victims in foreign countries may be due to a false perception, or wishful thinking, that some intervention is somehow taking place (or will take place soon) to save these foreign victims in foreign countries. Yet, the 'Good Samaritan' story clearly shows that, under fallen cultural norms and traditions, effective intervention on behalf of the victims may not take place from within.

In a way, the Good Samaritan put himself in the place of the victim, took a similar risk, and lifted the burden of the victim. The Samaritan's acts were not mere emotional responses at the spur of the moment; he visited the victim the next day, paid the extra expenses of taking care of him, and promised to return. He crossed cultural barriers and transformed fallen cultural norms. He did not follow or copy the fallen apathetic conduct of the Levite or the priest; instead, he initiated an ongoing redemptive intervention, saving the life of a 'foreign' victim, who, in the Biblical sense, was his neighbor.

---

[126] Indian media reported the refusal of some Christian missionaries, in a southern Tamil Nadu village, to help Hindu victims of the December 2004 Tsunami because they would not convert to Christianity (U.S. DOS, 2006a, Section 2d). If correct, this represents a clear violation of true Christian calling to help the victims (of fallen practices or natural crises) unconditionally. Furthermore, such unfortunate and fallen practices diminish the credibility and heighten the doubt about the intentions of future initiatives and interventions by Christian organizations.

Nevertheless, such interventions may stir opposition from all who gain at the expense of the enslaveables (and from transforming them into MDS victims). Therefore, such interventions entail the willingness to take on certain risks, such as social rejection – if helping the victims is against the prevailing norms and customs. Other risks include rejection and opposition from MDS perpetrators, and their collaborators who gain from such practices; possible rejection by the victims, since they have been tricked and deceived already by similar practices, or are misinformed and manipulated by their perpetrators; and, the risk of being harassed and persecuted.

The story of the Good Samaritan also highlights the importance of continued intervention to save the victims and care for their well-being. With regard to modern-day slavery, interventions should be part of an ongoing concern and participation; strong and ongoing intervention is crucial, especially in promoting continued interest in eradicating such appalling MDS practices. It is part of the ongoing long-term intervention to transform fallen practices – practices whose roots have been embedded for a very long time.

9. Jesus' direct care and concern for the victims and the poor: what Christians do for the victims and vulnerable is done for Jesus

"When the Son of Man comes in his glory, and all the angels with him, he will sit on his throne in heavenly glory. All the nations will be gathered before him, and he will separate the people one from another as a shepherd separates the sheep from the goats. He will put the sheep on his right and the goats on his left. "Then the King will say to those on his right, 'Come, you who are blessed by my Father; take your inheritance, the kingdom prepared for you since the creation of the world. For I was hungry and you gave me something to eat, I was thirsty and you gave me something to drink, I was a stranger and you invited me in, I needed clothes and you clothed me, I was sick and you looked after me, I was in prison and you came to visit me.' "Then the righteous will answer him, 'Lord, when did we see you hungry and feed you, or thirsty and give you something to drink? When did we see you a stranger and invite you in, or needing clothes and clothe you? When did we see you sick or in prison and go to visit you?' "The King will reply, 'I tell you the truth, whatever you did for one of the least of these brothers of mine, you did for me.' (Matthew 25: 31-40)

According to Matthew, when all nations gather before the Lord, the righteous will be rewarded for their good deeds toward the victims and vulnerable, who are hungry, thirsty, malnourished, strangers, sick, and/or persecuted. MDS victims and the enslaveables are typical examples of the least among us, whom the Lord calls His brothers and sisters. These victims come from all nations: anywhere and everywhere in the world, regardless of how far they are located, geographically, culturally, etc. The righteous, acting as active agents of renewal, behave according to the Lord's will, in response to the specific needs of the least of His brothers and sisters from all nations. They offer immediate help such as food and drink and clothing, hospitality for strangers, and attend to the needs of the sick, vulnerable, and persecuted. These are all typical needs of MDS victims and the enslaveables.

10. Remembering the pain and suffering of the victims

Remember those in prison as if you were their fellow prisoners, and those who are mistreated as if you yourselves were suffering. (Hebrews 13: 3)

Christians are called upon to have compassion and to care for the victims of oppression. Caring for the victims requires true understanding of the pain and suffering inflicted on such victims. If we imagine that we are the prisoners, the mistreated, the abused MDS victims, and the marginalized enslaveables, we would want to be remembered by others, hoping that someone will intervene on our behalf (Haugen, 1999, pp. 39-40). We are reminded to do the same for actual victims who suffer great pain and injustice.

11. Christians are called upon to build community with the marginalized and the oppressed

Keep on loving each other as brothers. Do not forget to entertain strangers, for by so doing some people have entertained angels without knowing it.

Remember those in prison as if you were their fellow prisoners, and those who are mistreated as if you yourselves were suffering. (Hebrew 13: 1-3)

Then Jesus said to his host, "When you give a luncheon or dinner, do not invite your friends, your brothers or relatives, or your rich neighbors; if you do, they may invite you back and so you will be repaid. But when you give a banquet, invite the poor, the crippled, the lame, the blind, and you will be blessed. Although they cannot repay you, you will be repaid at the resurrection of the righteous." (Luke 14: 12-14)

If one of your countrymen becomes poor and is unable to support himself among you, help him as you would an alien or a temporary resident, so he can continue to live among you. Do not take interest of any kind from him, but fear your God, so that your countryman may continue to live among you. You must not lend him money at interest or sell him food at a profit. (Leviticus 25: 35-37)

Called to be active agents of renewal, Christians should build and develop community with the marginalized and the oppressed, regardless of the whereabouts of these victims. Loving and caring for the poor and the oppressed will reverse the alienation of Christians from people who are forced, in this fallen world, to be marginalized and oppressed.

Christians should intervene, not only because of their concern for the truth, but also through love and compassion for the victims of fallen practices (Buechner, 1977, p. 8). Such love and compassion should reflect a close and ongoing relationship with a loving and compassionate God, who calls on us to do His work on Earth. Love and compassion for marginalized and oppressed victims will ensure ongoing and effective Christian interventions that will reverse their alienation and invite them into a loving and compassionate community where they are welcomed and treated equally as our brothers and sisters. Christians are called to follow moral norms that prompt them to take others' interests into account, especially the poor and vulnerable. Such moral norms are intrinsically rewarding norms that are valued for their own sake, even in the absence of external reward. Generalized moral norms that are extended to all individuals equally, will augment the social capital of the poor and vulnerable population.

Christians should augment such social capital, because it is good per se, and to counterpart the depreciation of generalized moral norms by the upper caste or the elite groups (Platteau, 1994b, pp. 766-771).

God commanded that we regard the poor and destitute, community members and aliens, with compassion. We are called, according to the Old Testament, to protect the destitute community-members, such as the widows and orphans (Exodus 22: 21-24; Deuteronomy 24: 17), and the physically disabled, such as the deaf and blind. We are also commanded to protect the aliens (Exodus 22:21, Deuteronomy 24: 17), not to show favoritism (Leviticus 19: 15), and not to profit at the expense of the poor and marginalized, and not to take advantage of their vulnerability and dire needs. "[25]If you lend money to one of my people among you who is needy, do not be like a moneylender; charge him no interest. [26] If you take your neighbor's cloak as a pledge, return it to him by sunset, [27] because his cloak is the only covering he has for his body. What else will he sleep in? When he cries out to me, I will hear, for I am compassionate" (Exodus 24: 25-27). God commands us to protect the basic human needs of the poor and marginalized and not to gain by making them more destitute, such as the enslaveables and MDS victims (Brown, 2004, pp. 104-106). The concerns and needs of the non-elite groups, especially the least among us, should be addressed and protected, instead of the fallen practices and traditions of favoring and attending to elite concerns, at the expense of the non-elite, including the destitute and marginalized groups.

Chapter 6
Summary and Conclusions

Institutions play a crucial role in spreading (or eradicating) certain practices, such as modern-day slavery, based on the societal reward/penalty systems that accompany such institutions. MDS practices tend to spread in societies and communities where informal institutions such as traditions and beliefs, sanction certain social behaviors and structures that separate and/or marginalize certain population groups, who do not satisfy such informal qualifications (e.g., the SC/ST in India). Formal institutions usually reflect the power structure and the influence of the winners of the existing informal institutions (e.g., the upper Hindu castes), at the expense of the vulnerable and marginalized (e.g., the SC/ST). Additionally, the governance structure of transactions, or contracts, usually works against enslaveables and MDS victims. Typically, MDS victims are less informed and more desperate, lack viable alternatives (or second sources), are intentionally marginalized to accept their fate as MDS victims, or become entrapped in sophisticated schemes and are forced to participate in MDS practices. In contrast, MDS perpetrators exploit the factors that further sustain their MDS practices. These factors include their information advantage, their ability to enhance their social capital and networks, and the waiting-game effect of outlasting and surviving interventions. The signaling effect also minimizes the effectiveness of intervention and heightens the fear and the submission of MDS victims and the enslaveables. Lastly, the interest-group effect serves the perpetrators' interests and the public-choice effect helps the perpetrators through corrupt government interventions – and deeming them ineffective. All of these factors contribute to the perpetrators' ability to sustain their MDS practices, reducing the risk of their involvement and increasing their share of the enslavement rent.

Furthermore, the new institutional economic analysis demonstrates the criteria for effective intervention against modern-day slavery. Effective interventions and remedies must respond to the causes, processes, and symptoms of modern-day slavery, and should take into consideration the different variables and participants that play significant roles in modern-day slavery. Due to the complexity of modern-day slavery, interventions should take place at the local, national, and international levels, and should cover immediate/short-term to long-term targets and objectives, taking into consideration the strengths and limitations of each level, form, and scope of intervention.

Immediate interventions should focus on rescuing and rehabilitating the current MDS victims, and prosecuting MDS perpetrators. Short-term interventions and remedies should focus on the governance structure of transactions, to reduce the information gap between MDS perpetrators and the enslaveables. Effective interventions should provide viable second sources to the former MDS victims and the enslaveables, such as schooling, employment, and credit and health clinic facilities. They should act as interest groups to provide legal and political support to MDS victims, to press for effective enforcement of existing anti-MDS laws, and to speak on behalf of the enslaveables and marginalized communities. Interventions should also provide the needed non-transferable assistance to MDS victims, such as education, training, and health services, using locally-produced forms of aid that are least likely to be transferred away from the enslaveables by MDS perpetrators or their collaborators. Furthermore, effective short-term interventions should aim to redirect public funds and foreign assistance toward community development, where the typical enslaveables live (in slums, shantytowns, and marginalized rural communities), supported by an effective presence of intervening agents who are willing to withstand such harsh environments (e.g., NGOs and CSOs).

Medium-term interventions should focus on influencing the existing formal rules by repealing existing laws that uphold discriminating practices, amending existing laws by closing loopholes and fixing vague rules, and by initiating new laws that prevent future schemes of MDS practices. Effective and ongoing interventions should empower the former enslaveables, level the playing field, and give them equal access to opportunities available to others, such as proportional participation and representation in administrative, legislative, and judicial bodies at all levels (local, state and national).

Long-term interventions should aim to reverse the course of unjust embedded norms and traditions (informal institutions) and repealing the unjust laws and traditions (formal institutions). Such processes may take decades or centuries. The gradual impact of such intervention requires sustained involvement of NGOs and CSOs that are willing to maintain their presence, and exert the effort to make gradual changes in inherited informal institutions.

The book proposes a set of special considerations associated with foreign and international interventions against MDS practices in LDCs, to enhance the effectiveness of such interventions. Foreign and international interventions should realize that the poor are people, and not countries. Therefore, foreign and international assistance should be designed to help the poor, marginalized communities, and victims of existing/inherited, discriminating, institutional environments. Foreign aid and assistance programs should be designed carefully to avoid and deter the practices of transferring such aid away from the poor and marginalized communities, and to be guarded with an effective presence (e.g., NGOs) in these communities.

Foreign and international interventions should be perceptive to embedded "sacred" beliefs, especially controversial ones, to keep away from potential propaganda by MDS perpetrators and their collaborators, who may demonize the intention of foreign and international interventions and thwart their efforts against

MDS practices. Consequently, foreign and international interventions should be transparent, with clear agendas that focus primarily on serving the interests of MDS victims and the enslaveables. Furthermore, foreign and international interventions should oppose discriminating institutional environments, such as discriminating informal norms and rules, and seek to level the playing field, with regard to human rights practices. Integral components of their interventions should include the application of the United Nations' Universal Declaration of Human Rights and other related international human rights' laws, conventions, and declarations for all people. Lastly, international intervention should rethink or postpone a worldwide ban on trading goods produced by child labor until viable second sources are available and effective for improving the well-being of these child laborers. Lack of such second sources is likely to expose these laborers to worse forms of MDS schemes and practices.

The book concludes with a Biblical perspective on modern-day slavery, and highlights the foundations for effective Christian interventions and remedies that address MDS practices and respond to their causes and symptoms, for the purpose of transforming such practices and redeeming their victims. First, Christians should express special care for the victims, treating them as our neighbors – regardless of the geographic, national, or cultural barriers. Second, Christian interventions should be watchful of MDS schemes to counterbalance them, by investing in information and knowledge regarding such practices, and to intervene wisely, focusing always on the main goal – to rescue MDS victims and empower the enslaveables. Third, Christians should search for and identify the victims (MDS victims) and the vulnerable (the enslaveables) who are typically voiceless and defenseless. Fourth, Christian interventions should reflect the role of Christians as faithful servants, with a persistent presence, and by serving the interests of the victims as reliable second sources and interest groups, despite harsh environments and the risks involved. Effective Christian interventions should take place even in hostile environments, or, if a Christian presence is not permitted or tolerated, through partnership and alliances with other indigenous organizations having strong anti-MDS profiles and proven records of assistance to the poor. Fifth, Christians should not hesitate to act against the perpetrators, void their schemes, directly, or indirectly, and serve as watchdogs, informing and cooperating with authorities and other interested organizations to prosecute the perpetrators and to prevent further oppressive practices. Sixth, Christian interventions should be ongoing, to outlast the perpetrators and their schemes, and to gain the trust of the victims. Seventh, Christian intervention should be insightful, to avoid any cultural taboos or barriers that could be exploited by the perpetrators and their collaborators – against Christian or foreign interventions. Eighth, Christian intervention should also choose shrewdly the forms of aid and assistance given to the victims and the enslaveables, using the least-transferable aid to the victims and the enslaveables. Lastly, Christian organizations should learn from the expertise and successful records of other organizations and coordinate with them whenever appropriate, to assure effective interventions, and by complementing existing organizations' interventions, and using available resources wisely.

Bibliography

Abraham, Anita and Jean-Philippe Platteau (2001) "Participatory Development in the Presence of Endogenous Community Imperfections." worldbank.org/INTABCDEWASHINGTON2001/Resources/abraham.pdf.

Akerlof, George A., (1976) "The Economics of Caste and of the Rat Race and Other Woeful Tales," The Quarterly Journal of Economics 90(4): 599-617.

Akerlof, George A. and William T. Dickens (1982) "The Economic Consequences of Cognitive Dissonance," American Economic Review, vol. 72(3): 307-319.

Axelrod, Robert A. (1986) An Evolutionary Approach to Norms. American Political Science Review 80(4): 1095-1111.

Anti-Slavery International. (1997) India – Bonded Labour: the Gap between Illusion and Reality. UN Submissions 1997 <http://www.antislavery.org/archive/submission/submission1997-08India.htm>.

_____. (2002) Manual Scavenging - The Most Indecent Form of Work. UN Submissions 2002. <http://www.antislavery.org/archive/submission/submission2002-scavenging.htm>.

Bales, Kevin (1999) Disposable People: New Slavery in the Global Economy. California: University of California Press.

Barrett, Christopher B. and Brant M. Swallow (2006), "Fractal Poverty Traps," World Development, 34 (1): 1-15.

Basu, Kaushik (1999) "Child Labor: Cause, Consequence and Cure with Remarks on International Labor Standards," Journal of Economic Literature 37(3): 1083-1119.

_____. (1986) One Kind of Power. Oxford Economic Papers. New Series 38(2):259-282

Bauer, Péter T., (1981) Equality, the Third World and Economic Delusion. Cambridge, Mass: Harvard University Press.

Bayly, Susan (1999) Caste, Society and Politics in India from the Eighteen Century to the Modern Age. The New Cambridge History of India IV.3. Cambridge: Cambridge University Press.

164

Beaulier, Scott A., Peter J. Boettke, and Christopher J. Coyne (2005) "Knowledge, Economics, and Coordination: Understanding Hayek's Legal Theory." NYU Journal of Law & Liberty 1 (0): 209-223.

Becker, Gary (1995) "The Economic Way of Looking at Behavior." In Ramon Febrero and Pedro Schwartz (Eds) The Essence of Becker. Stanford, CA: Hoover Institution Press: 633-658.

Berreman, Gerald D (1966) "Caste and Community Development." In William Rowe (Ed) Contours of Culture Change in South Asia. Monograph number 9. Reprint of Human Organization, Vol. 22, No. 1, 1963. Lexington, Kentucky: The Society for Applied Anthropology: 90-94.

Bloch, Francis, and Vijayendra Rao (2000) "Terror as a Bargaining Instrument: A Case Study of Dowry Violence in Rural India." Policy Research working paper. Report # 2347, The World Bank Group, May 2000.

Bondurant, Joan. (1966) "Traditional Polity and the Dynamics of Change in India." In William Rowe (Ed) Contours of Culture Change in South Asia. Monograph number 9. Reprint of Human Organization, Vol. 22, No. 1, 1963. Lexington, Kentucky: The Society for Applied Anthropology: 5-10

Bowles, Samuel (1998) "Endogenous Preferences: The Cultural Consequences of market and other Economic Institutions." Journal of Economic Literature, XXXVI: 75-111.

Brehm, Jack (1956) "Postdecision Changes in the Desirability of Alternatives," Journal of Abnormal Social Psychology, May 1956, 52: 384-89.

Brown, Patricia Gates (2004) Free People: A Christian Response to Global Economics. USA: Xlibris.

Buchanan, James (2003) "Public Choice: Politics without Romance." Policy. 19-3 (Spring 2003): 13-18 <http://www.cis.org.au/Policy/spr03/polspr03-2.htm>.

Buchanan, James M. and Gordon Tullock (1967). The Calculus of Consent: Logical Foundation of Constitutional Democracy. Ann Arbor, MI: The University of Michigan Press, second printing.

Buechner, Frederick (1977) Telling the truth: The Gospel as Tragedy, Comedy & Fairy Tale. San Francisco: HarperCollin.

Bulsara, Shiraz, and Priyadarshini Sreenivasa (2003-04) "Driven to Bondage and Starvation." Combat Law 2(5) (2003-04) < http://www.indiatogether.org/combatlaw/vol2/issue5/bondage.htm>.

Cancian, Frank (1966) Maximization as Norm, Strategy, and Theory: A Comment on Programmatic Statements in Economic Anthropology. American Anthropologist, New Series, 8(2): 465-470

CBS News. (2000) 60 Minutes II. Tobacco Slaves in India. 29 August 2000 <http://www.cbsnews.com/stories/1999/11/22/60II/main71386.shtml#August>.

_____. (2001) Modern-day Slavery. 12 July 2001 <http://www.cbsnews.com/stories/2001/07/12/opinion/diplomatic/main30 1205.shtml>.

Census of India. (1991 and 2001) <http://www.censusindia.net>.

Chakma, Suhas (Ed) (2007) India Human Rights Report 2006. New Delhi, India: Asian Centre for Human Rights (ACHR).

Chopra, Anuj (2006) India's latest move to stop child labor. The Christian Science Monitor, October 10, 2006 <http://www.csmonitor.com/2006/1010/p07s02-wosc.html>.

CIA. The World Factbook: India <http://www.cia.gov/cia/publications/factbook/geos/in.html>.

Coalition Against Trafficking in Women <http://www.catwinternational.org/>.

Coleman, James (1987) "Norms as Social Capital." In Gerald Radnitzky and Pater Bernholz (Eds) Economic Imperialism: The Economics Method Applied Outside the Field of Economics. New York: Paragon House Publishers: 133-53.

Commons, John (1931) "Institutional Economics." American Economic Review 21: 648-657.

Cooper, Ben, Cecilia Garcia-Peñalosa, and Peter Funk (2001). "Status Effects and Negative Utility Growth," Economic Journal, Royal Economic Society 111(473): 642-65.

Coursen-Neff, Zama. (2003) "For 15 Million in India, a Childhood of Slavery MEANWHILE." International Herald Tribune 31 January 2003 <http://www.hrw.org/editorials/2003/india013103.htm>.

Dandhua Mukti Morcha (The Bonded Labour Liberation Movement). Slavery.. A Continuing Human Tragedy <http://www.swamiagnivesh.com/phamp.htm>.

Das, Veena. (1982) Structure and Cognition: Aspects of Hindu Caste and Ritual. Second Edition. Delhi: Oxford University Press.

Das Gupta, Monica and Li Shuzhuo. (1999) "Gender Bias in China, South Korea and India, 1920-1990: Effects of War, Famine and Fertility Decline." Development and Change 30(3): 619-652

Das Gupta, Monica et al. (2000) "State Policies and Women's Autonomy in China, the Republic of Korea, and India 1950-2000: Lessons from Contrasting Experiences." World Bank Working Paper. Report #21743. Washington, DC: World Bank .

Dayan, Joelle, Anna-Beth Doyle, and Dorothy Markiewicz (2001) "Social support networks and self-esteem of idiocentric and allocentric children and adolescents." Journal of Social and Personal Relationships 18(6): 767-784.

De Bary, William Theodore (1998). Asian Values and Human Rights: A Confucian Communitarian perspective. Massachusetts: Harvard University Press.

Dean, Judith (2005) "Why Trade Matters for the Poor." In Judith Dean, Julie Schaffner, and Stephen Smith (Eds) Attacking Poverty in the Developing World: Christian Practitioners and Academics in Collaboration. Waynesboro, GA: Authentic: 253-267.

Denzau, Arthur and Douglass North. (1993) "Shared Mental Models: Ideologies and Institutions" Economic History 9309003, Economics Working Paper Archive at WUSTL <http://econwpa.wustl.edu/eps/eh/papers/9309/9309003.pdf>.

Deshpande, Ashwini (2000) "Does Caste Stile Define Disparity? A Look at Inequality in Kerala, India." The American Economic Review 90(2): 322-325.

Djankov, Simeon, Jose Garcia-Montalvo, and Marta Reynal-Querol (2006a) "Does Foreign Aid Help?" (March 2006). Available at SSRN: http://ssrn.com/abstract=896550

_____. (2006b) "The Curse of Aid" (March 2006). Available at SSRN: http://ssrn.com/abstract=893558

Dugger, William (1995) "Douglass C. North New Institutionalism." Journal of Economic Issues XXIX: 454-458

The Economist (1995a) "India's Rich Little Poor Girls" (334): 40.

_____. (1995b) "Consciences and Consequences." (335)7917: 13-14.

_____. (1996) "The flourishing business of slavery" (340)7984: 43-44.

Elster, Jon (1989) "Social Norms and Economic Theory." Journal of Economic Perspectives 3(4): 99-117.

Embassy of India. India Information <http://www.indianembassy.org/indiainfo/index.html>.

Fafchamps Marcel (2004) Market Institutions in Sub Saharan Africa: Theory and Evidence. Cambridge, Mass: The MIT Press.

Fafchamps, Marcel and Forhad Shilpi (2005) "Cities and Specialization : Evidence from South Asia." Economic Journal 115(503): 477-504.

Fafchamps, Marcel and Jackline Wahba. (2006) Child Labor, Urban Proximity and Household Composition. IZA Discussion Paper No.1966. Accessed 10 March 2006 <http://ssrn.com/abstract=882822>.

Free The Slaves <http://www.freetheslaves.net/resources/links.html>.

Freeman, James M. (1979) Untouchable: An Indian Life History. Stanford: Stanford University Press.

Galasso, Emanuela and Martin Ravallion (2000) "Distributional Outcomes of a Decentralized Welfare Program," Policy Research Working Paper 2316, World Bank.

Gentleman, Amelia (2006) "Indian ban on child labor: Who will clean the houses?" International Herald Tribune, September 6, 2006 <http://www.iht.com/articles/2006/09/06/news/letter.php>.

Goonesekere, Rajendra (2001) Prevention of Discrimination and Protection of Indigenous Peoples and Minorities. World Conference against Racism (WCAR). E/CN.4/Sub.2/2001/16. 13 Aug 2001 <http://wcar.alrc.net/mainfile.php/Documents/48/>.

Gopakumar, K. (1998) "Citizen Feedback Surveys to Highlights Corruption in Public Services: The experience of Public Affairs Centre, Bangalore." Working Paper. Transparency International.

Granovetter, Mark (1985) Economic Action and Social Structure: The Problem of Embeddedness. American Journal of Sociology 91(3):481-510.

_____. (1991) "The Social Construction of Economic Institutions." In Amitai Etzioni and Paul Lawrence (Eds) Socio-economics: Toward a New Synthesis, Amonk, NY, M.E. Sharpe: 38-84

Grindle, Merilee and John Thomas (1991) Public Choices and Policy Change: The Political Economy of Reform in Developing Countries. Baltimore: Johns Hopkins University.

Guinnane, Timothy (2005). "Trust: A Concept Too Many," Working Papers 907, Economic Growth Center, Yale University.

Gupta, Akhil. (1995) "Blurred Boundaries: The Discourse of Corruption, the Culture of Politics and the Imagined State." American Ethnologist. 22(2): 375-402.

Guru, Gopal. (2004) "Dalit Vision of India: from Bahiskhurt to Inclusive Bharat." Future 36(6-7): 757-763.

Haidar, Suhasini.(2003) Dowry-Busting bride wins star status. CNN. 23 May 2003 <http://www.cnn.com/2003/WORLD/asiapcf/south/05/23/india.dowry/>

Harris, John, Janet Hunter, and Colin Lewis (Eds.) The New Institutional Economics and Third World Development. New York: Routledge, 1998 (Reprint).

Hasnat, Baban (1995) "International Trade and Child Labor." Journal of Economic Issues, XXIX: 419-426.

Haugen, Gary (1999) Good News about Injustice: A witness of Courage in a Hurting World. Downers Grove, IL: InterVarsity Press.

Hill, J.P. (1999) Public Choice: A Review. Faith & Economics 34:1-10.

Hirsch, Fred (1976). Social limits to Growth. Cambridge, MA: Harvard University Press.

Hirschman, Albert (1982) "Rival Interpretations of Market Society: Civilizing, Destructive or Feeble?" Journal of Economic Literature 20 (4): 1463-1484.

Hoksbergen, Roland (1999) "Give them a Fish, Teach them to Fish, or Organize a Fishing Club? NGOs, Civil Societies and Economic Development." Faith & Economics 34: 11-18.

_____. (2005) "Partnering with Local Organizations in Poverty Reduction Efforts." In Judith Dean, Julie Schaffner, and Stephen Smith (Eds) Attacking Poverty in the Developing World: Christian Practitioners and Academics in Collaboration. Waynesboro, GA: Authentic: 187-198.

Human Rights Watch (1999) Broken People: Caste Violence Against India's "Untouchables." <http://www.hrw.org/reports/1999/india/>.

_____. (2003 and 2005) World Reports 2003 and 2005: India <http://hrw.org/doc/?t=asia&c=india>.

_____. (2003b) Small Changes: Bonded Child Labor in India's Silk Industry <http://www.hrw.org/reports/2003/india/india0103.pdf>.

_____. (1996) The Small Hands of Slavery: Bonded Child Labor In India <http://hrw.org/reports/1996/India3.htm>.

International Bible Society (1984). The Holy Bible: New International Version (NIV). Grand Rapids, MI: Zondervan.

International Justice Mission < http://www.ijm.org/>.

ILO (2005) Child Labor and Response: Overview Note – India. International Programme on the Elimination of Child Labour <http://www.ilo.org/public/english/region/asro/newdelhi/ipec/responses/india/index.htm>.

_____. (2001). CEACR: Individual Observation concerning Convention No. 29, Forced Labour, 1930 India (ratification: 1954) <http://www.ilo.org/ilolex/english/newcountryframeE.htm>.

Jaffrelot, Christophe (2003) India's Silent Revolution: The Rise of the Lower Castes in Northern India. New York: Columbian University Press.

Jacobs, Charles (1996) "Slavery: Worldwide Evil." The World & I. The American Anti-Slavery Group <http://www.iabolish.com/today/background/worldwide-evil.htm>.

Jeffrey, Craig (2002) "Caste, Class, and Clientelism: A political economy of Everyday Corruption in Rural North India." Economic Geography 78 (1): 21-42.

Johnson, Jerker and Hans Blomqvist (1996) "Development Aid - An Object for International Rent Seeking?" Proceedings of the University of Vaasa,

Discussion Papers 204. Available at SSRN: http://ssrn.com/abstract=38049

Kasper, Wolfgang, and Manfred Streit (1998) Institutional Economics: Social Order and Public Policy. Massachusetts: Edward Elgar Publishing Limited.

Kaufman, Bruce E (2007) "The institutional economics of John R. Commons: complement and substitute for neoclassical economic theory." Socio-Economic Review 5(1): 3-45; doi:10.1093/ser/mwl016.

Khan, Mushtaq (1996) "The efficiency implications of corruption." Journal of International Development 8(5): 683-696.

Knox, Robert E., and James Inkster A. (1968) "Postdecisions Dissonance at Post Time," Journal of Personality and Social Psychology, April 1968, 1(8): 319-23.

Kolenda, Pauline (1966) "Toward a Model of the Hindu Jajmani System." In William Rowe (Ed) Contours of Culture Change in South Asia. Monograph number 9. Reprint of Human Organization, Vol. 22, No. 1, 1963. Lexington, Kentucky: The Society for Applied Anthropology: 11-31.

Konow, James. (2000) "Fair Shares: Accountability and Cognitive Dissonance in Allocation Decisions." The American Economic Review 90 (4): 1072-1091.

Korobkin, Russell B. (2003) "Bounded Rationality, Standard Form Contracts, and Unconscionability." University of Chicago Law Review 70:1203-1295.

Krishna, Anirudh. (2003) "What is Happening to Caste? A View from Some North Indian Villages." The Journal of Asian Studies. 62(4): 1171-1194.

Krueger, Anne (1974) "The Political Economy of the Rent-Seeking Society." The American Economic Review 64(3) 291:303

Kunreuther, Howard et al. (1978) Disaster Insurance Protection: Public Policy Lessons. New York: : John Wiley & Son.

Lambsdorff, Jonathan G. (2002) Framework Document 2002: Background Paper to the 2002 Corruption Perceptions Index. Transparency International (TI) and Göttingen University.

Lewis, Oscar (1965) Village life in northern India; studies in a Delhi village. New York: Vintage Books.

Lim, Lin Lean (1998) "Child Prostitution." In Lim, Lin Lean (Ed) The Sex Sector: The Economic and Social Bases of Prostitution in Southeast Asia. Geneva: International Labour Office: 170-205.

Lipset, Seymour and Gabriel Lenz (2000) "Corruption, Cultures, and Markets." In Lawrence Harrison and Samuel Huntington (Eds) Culture Matters: How Values Shape Human Progress. New York: Basic Books: 112-124.

Luke, Nancy and Kaivan Munshi (2004) Women as Agents of Change: Female Incomes and Household Decisions in South India. BREAD Working Paper No. 087.

Luschinsky, Mildred (1966) "Problem of Cultural Change in the Indian Village." In William Rowe (Ed) Contours of Culture Change in South Asia. Monograph number 9. Reprint of Human Organization, Vol. 22, No. 1, 1963. Lexington, Kentucky: The Society for Applied Anthropology: 66-74.

Madison, Gary Brent (1998) The political economy of civil society and human rights. London: Routledge.

Marshall, Katherine (2005) Development Challenges for the New Millennium: Dialogue and Partnership Issues for Faith and Development Institutions." In Judith Dean, Julie Schaffner, and Stephen Smith (Eds) Attacking Poverty in the Developing World: Christian Practitioners and Academics in Collaboration. Waynesboro, GA: Authentic: 241-251.

McChesney, Fred (1997) Money for Nothing: Politicians, Rent-Extraction, and Political Extortion. Cambridge, MA: Harvard University Press.

_____. (1987) "Rent Extraction and Rent Creation in the Economic Theory of Regulation." Journal of Legal Studies (16): 10–18.

Mendelsohn, Oliver and Marika Vicziany (1998) The Untouchables: Subordination, Poverty and the State in Modern India. Cambridge: Cambridge University Press, 1998.

Ministry of Human Resource Development (2001-2002) Department of Elementary Education & Literacy and Department Secondary and Higher Educations. Annual Report 2001-2002. Government of India <http://shikshanic.nic.in/cd50years/ar2002/ar01_02.pdf>.

Noll, Roger (1988) "The politics of Regulations." In Richard Schmalensee (Ed) Handbook of Industrial Organization. The Netherlands: Elsevier Science Publishers B.V.: 1254-1287.

North, Douglass (2000) "Economic Institutions and Development: A view from the Bottom." In Mancur Olson and Satu Kähkönen (Eds) A Not-So-Dismal Science: A Broader View of Economics and Societies. New York: Oxford University Press: 92-118.

_____. (2002) The New Institutional Economics and Development, Washington University, St. Louis. Paper available at <http://www.econ.iastate.edu/tesfatsi/NewInstE.North.pdf>.

_____. (1994) "Economic Performance through Time." The American Economic Review. 84:3 59-368.

_____. (1990) Institutions, Institutional Change and Economic Performance. Cambridge: Cambridge University Press.

_____. (1998) "The New Institutional Economics and Third World Development." In John Harris, Janet Hunter, and Colin Lewis (Eds) The New Institutional Economics and Third World Development. New York: Routledge: 17-26.

Nussbaum, Martha C. (2000) Women and Human Development: The Capabilities Approach. Cambridge (UK): Cambridge University Press.

Ogilvie, Sheilagh (2004) How Does Social Capital Affect Women? Guilds and Communities in Early Modern Germany. The American Historical Review 109.2 (2004): 65 pars. 13 Feb. 2006 <http://www.historycooperative.org/journals/ahr/109.2/ogilvie.html>.

Orenstein, Henry (1966) "Village, Caste, and the Welfare State." In William Rowe (Ed) Contours of Culture Change in South Asia. Monograph number 9. Reprint of Human Organization, Vol. 22, No. 1, 1963. Lexington, Kentucky: The Society for Applied Anthropology, 83-89.

Overdorf, Jason. (2003) "Criminal Conversion." Far Eastern Economic Review. 166.37 (September 18, 2003) <http://www.fsa.ulaval.ca/personnel/vernag/EH/F/cause/lectures/Criminal %20Conversions.htm>.

Osterfeld, David (1994) "The World Bank and the IMF: Misbegotten Sisters." In Peter Boettke (Ed) The Collapse of Development planning: the Political Economy Of The Austrian School. New York: New Your University Press: 185-209.

Pandey, Geeta (2006) India Tightens Child Labor Laws. BBC News <http://news.bbc.co.uk/2/low/south_asia/6034335.stm.>.

Platteau, Jean-Philippe (1994a). Behind the Market Stage Where Real Societies Exist- Part I: The Role of Public and Private Institutions. The Journal of Development Studies 30(3): 533-577.

_____. (1994b). Behind the Market Stage Where Real Societies Exist- Part II: The Role of Moral Norms. The Journal of Development Studies 30(3): 753-817.

Ravallion, Martin and Dominique van de Walle (2001) Breaking up the Collective Farm: Welfare Outcomes of Viet Nam's Massive Land Privatization. World Bank: Washington D.C.

Rawls, John (1993) Political Liberalism. New York: Columbia University Press.

Rowe, William J. (1966) "Changing Rural Class Structures and the Jajmani System." In William Rowe (Ed) Contours of Culture Change in South Asia. Monograph number 9. Reprint of Human Organization, Vol. 22, No.

172

1, 1963. Lexington, Kentucky: The Society for Applied Anthropology, 41-44.

Saintsbury, George (1972) East India Slavery. Second edition. London: Charles Tilt, 1829. Reprinted in Ireland: Irish University Press.

Sawyer, Roger (1986) Slavery in the Twentieth Century. New York: Routledge & Kegan Paul.

Sen, Amartya (1999) Development as Freedom. New York: Anchor Books.

_____. (2002) Rationality and Freedom. Harvard: Harvard Belknap Press.

Srinivas, Mysore (1966). Social Change in Modern India. Berkeley: University of California Press.

Streeten, Paul (1981) "Development Ideas in Historical perspective." In Paul Streeten (Ed) Development Perspectives. New York: St. Martin's Press.

_____. (1998) "Beyond the Six Veils: Conceptualizing and Measuring Poverty."Journal of International Affairs. 52: 1-31.

Svensson, Jakob (2000) "Foreign Aid and Rent-Seeking." Journal of International Economics 51:437–461

Swinnerton, Kenneth and Carol Ann Rogers (1999). "The Economics of Child Labor: Comment." American Economic Review 89(3): 1382-1385.

Sykuta, Michael E. and Michael L. Cook (2001) A New Institutional Economics Approach to Contracts and Cooperatives. American Journal of Agricultural Economics 83(1) 1273:1279

Thorat, Sukhadev (2002) "Hindu Social Order and the Human Right of Dalits." Combat Law 1(4) <http://www.indiatogether.org/combatlaw/issue4/hinduorder.htm>.

Todaro, Michael and Stephen Smith (2006) Economic Development. Ninth edition. Massachusetts: Pearson Addison-Wesley

Transparency International (2006) Corruption Perceptions Index 2006. <http://www.transparency.org/policy_research/surveys_indices/cpi/2006>.

Triandis, Harry (1995). Individualism & Collectivism. Boulder: Westview Press.

Triandis, Harry and David Trafimow (2001) "Cross-National Prevalence of Collectivism." In Constantine Sedikides and Marilynn Brewer (Eds) Individual Self, Relational Self, Collective Self. Philadelphia: Psychology press: 259-276.

UNESCO (2002) Universal Declaration on Cultural Diversity. <http://www.unesco.org/education/imld_2002/unversal_decla.shtml#2>

United Nations (2000) Committee on Elimination of Discrimination Against Women Continues Consideration of India Report. Press Release WOM/1162, January 24, 2000 <http://www.un.org/News/Press/docs/2000/20000124.wom1162.doc.html>.

_____. (1957) <u>Supplementary Convention on the Abolition of Slavery, the Slave Trade, and Institutions and Practices Similar to Slavery.</u> High Commissioner for human Rights, 30 April 1957 <http://www.unhchr.ch/html/menu3/b/30.htm>.

_____. (1948) <u>Universal Declaration of Human Rights.</u> High Commissioner for human Rights. General Assembly resolution 217A (III) of December 10, 1948 <http://www.unhchr.ch/udhr/lang/eng.htm>.

_____. (undated) International Human Rights Instruments. High Commissioner for human Rights < http://www.unhchr.ch/html/intlinst.htm> accessed 8 February 2007.

UNDP (2006). <u>Human Development Report 2006: Beyond Scarcity: Power, Poverty and the Global Water Crisis</u> <http://hdr.undp.org/hdr2006/report.cfm>

_____. (2004a). <u>Human Development Report 2004: Cultural liberty in today's diverse world.</u> 2004 <http://hdr.undp.org/reports/global/2004/>.

_____. (2004b) <u>How to Define and Measure Extreme Poverty</u> <http://www.undp.org.my/uploads/files/How%20to%20define%20and%20measure%20extreme%20poverty.pdf> accessed June 30 2006.

_____. (Undated) Millennium Development Goals-MDGs <http://www.undp.org/mdg/>

UNICEF (2004) The State of the World Children 2005: Childhood Under Threat. New York, UNICEF House

Unni, Jeemol (2001) <u>Earnings and Education among Ethnic Groups in Rural India.</u> National Council of Applied Economic Research. Working Paper No. 79. New Delhi, India.

U.S. DOS (2000a-2007a) <u>India: Country Report on Human Rights Practices.</u> Annual Reports 1999 - 2006 <http://www.state.gov/g/drl/rls/hrrpt/>.

U.S. DOS (2001b-2006b) <u>Victims of Trafficking and Violence Protection Act 2000: Trafficking in Persons Report.</u> 2001-2006 Reports <http://www.state.gov/g/tip/rls/tiprpt/>.

U.S. DOS (2004c) Mauritania<u>: Country Report on Human Rights Practices.</u> Annual Report 2004 <http://www.state.gov/g/drl/rls/hrrpt/2004/41615.htm>.

U.S. DOS (2004d) Sudan<u>: Country Report on Human Rights Practices.</u> Annual Report 2004 <http://www.state.gov/g/drl/rls/hrrpt/2004/41628.htm>.

Walz-Chojnacki, Greg (1999) <u>Markos Mamalakis: The Man behind 'Mesoeconomics'</u> <http://www.uwm.edu/News/report/old/april99/people.html>.

174

Weiner, Myron (1991) The Child and the State in India: Child Labor and Education Policy in Comparative Perspective. New Jersey: Princeton University Press.

Wiesel, Elie (1986) The Nobel Acceptance Speech Delivered by Elie Wiesel in Oslo on December 10, 1986 <http://www.eliewieselfoundation.org/ElieWiesel/Nobel_Speech.htm>.

Williamson, Oliver (2000) "The New Institutional Economics: Taking Stock, Looking Ahead." Journal of Economic Literature XXXVIII: 595-613.

_____. (1993). "Calculativeness, Trust, and Economic Organization." Journal of Law and Economics 36(1), part 2, pp.453-486

_____. (1981). "The Economies of Organization: The Transaction Cost Approach". American Journal of Sociology. 87: 548—577

The World Bank. India: Data and Statistics <Http://worldbank.org/in>.

_____. (2006) World Development Indicators 2006. Washington D.C., The World Bank.

_____. (2001) World Development Report 2000/2001: Attacking Poverty. New York: Oxford University Press.

Wright, Marcia (1993) Strategies of slaves & women: Life-Stories from East/Central Africa. New York: Lilian Barber Press.

Zoba, Wendy M. (1999) "Good News for the Lost, Imprisoned, Abducted, and Enslaved." Christianity Today 43: 35-43.

Index